**What Others Are Saying about This Book:**

"Who are educators, and what do they do? This innovative book tells the story of twenty-two nontraditional educational pioneers. At a time when educational leadership has never been more important, the profiles provide insight and inspiration for all who care about the education of America's youth."

— *Madeleine Wing Adler, President*
*West Chester University*

"I know and admire several of the people described in this book. Their inspiring stories may give you a new perspective on schooling and the roles available to educators."

— *Ron Brandt, Executive Editor Emeritus*
Educational Leadership
*Association of Supervision and Curriculum Development*

"A literary quilt: individuals of strength, vignettes of character, stories of commitment. You'll enjoy every chapter."

— *Bob Caine, Superintendent*
*Kentfield School District*

"This book helps to dispel our apprehensions about a competitive education industry by introducing us to some of the good and dedicated people who make it up. It shows how these entrepreneurs, far from excluding difficult-to-educate children, often build their businesses around serving them, and it reveals a far higher degree of flexibility and responsiveness to customer demand out in the public sector. Read *The Educational Entrepreneur* if you would like a glimpse at the future of education."

— *Andrew J. Coulson, Author*
Market Education: The Unknown History

"People interested in the improvement of teaching and learning will find this book fascinating."

*William Cunningham*
*Former Assistant to the Governor*
*for Education, California*

"As the twentieth century saw the emergence of a new economy that was driven by the entrepreneur, the 21st century will see the emergence of the new educational paradigm, public-private partnerships that will be led by a new class of innovator: the educational entrepreneur. Don Leisey and Charles Lavaroni have turned their analytic spotlight on this new phenomenon and produced what may become a landmark work."

*— Jerome S. Engel, Executive Director*
*Lester Center for Entrepreneurship*
*Haas School of Business*
*University of California, Berkeley*

"This book provides some fascinating insights into the lives of people who have created businesses that have made positive changes in the lives of teachers and students."

*— Carolyn Horan, Director*
*Buck Institute for Educational Research and Evaluation*

"The creativity, vision, and resourcefulness of educational entrepreneurs are changing the face of our educational system. Moreover, the entrepreneurial efforts of women and men like those whose successes are described in this book are destined to shape our educational future. I congratulate the authors of this new book and extend a special thanks to them for sharing these stories."

*— Marilyn Kourilsky, Vice President*
*Kauffman Center for Entrepreneurial Leadership*

"This book is especially interesting for all people who might be looking to find new sources of personal energy to bring to teaching and learning."

*— Linda Lambert, Professor*
*California State University at Hayward*
*Author,* Building Leadership Capacity in Schools

"Teachers reading this book are bound to get some ideas about the future of education and their possible roles in it. A must read for the people who are thinking about their own creativity and commitment to learning."

*— David Martin, Professor of Education*
*Gallaudet University*

"Educational entrepreneurship is an idea whose time has come. Books like this that celebrate the achievements of the champions of education renewal fill a vital gap in the change process of both private and public endeavors. This book details the victories of successful entrepreneurs and teaches us how to protect and nurture those champions who will follow them."

*— William Martin, Principal*
*Monroe High School*

"Entrepreneurship has been the cornerstone for the remarkable growth of our economy and our country. Encouraging innovative entrepreneurs in the education field will build on this heritage and improve the quality of American education."

*— Robert Ohrenschall, Founder*
*Ohrenschall Center for Entrepreneurship*
*San Francisco State University*

"Leisey and Lavaroni have introduced all of us to a group of educators who have made important linkages between what they believe and the successful businesses they have created. They have shown us the way to connect problems with opportunity."

*— Carol Sager, Director*
*Center for Essential Linkages and Learning*

"Chuck Lavaroni and Don Leisey's book, *The Educational Entrepreneur,* adds a new perspective and makes a valuable contribution to the field of education."

*— Franklin Schargel, The Schargel Consulting Group*
*Author,* Transforming Education Through Total Quality Management *and* Dropout Proofing Schools

"Leisey and Lavaroni have identified a new category of entrepreneurs — educators who have created new investment opportunities for people who are interested not only in their own financial growth, but in the improvement of society as well."

*— Tom Thorner, Managing Partner*
*Thorner Ventures*

"This book will cause teachers contemplating a departure from the classroom to reconsider and perhaps rededicate their creative energies, as their peers have so dramatically done with entrepreneurial endeavors, to solve educational problems within our existing educational environment."

*— F. Robert Walczak, Executive Director*
*Computer Using Educators (CUE)*

"Today's teachers will find the lives of the people reviewed in this book both thought provoking and inspirational."

*— Elaine Wilson Rosenfield, Kindergarten Teacher*
*Former California Educator of the Year*

"An inspiring set of case studies of self-made entrepreneurs in the growing education industry. This is the PROFILES IN COURAGE book for educators who aspire to break the stifling bonds of employment in someone else's shop, to own and grow the shop themselves."

*— Dennis C. Zuelke, Professor*
*Jacksonville State University*
*Author,* Educational Private Practice

# The Educational Entrepreneur

# The Educational Entrepreneur

## Making a Difference

Donald E. Leisey, EdD, and Charles Lavaroni, MS

delaplus@aol.com
www.edenterpreneurs.org

San Rafael, California

Editor: Ellen Kleiner
Book design and production: Pete Masterson, www.aeonix.com
Cover design and production: Caroline Garrett
Authors' photo: Michael Mendelson



Published by: Edupreneur Press
DEL Tower
21 Silk Oak Circle
San Rafael, CA 94901

Printed in the United States of America on acid-free recycled paper

**Publisher's Cataloging-in-Publication Data**

Leisey, Donald E.
The educational entrepreneur: making a difference / Donald E. Leisey and Charles Lavaroni. — 1st ed.
p. cm.
Includes bibliographical references.
LCCN: 99-97750
ISBN: 0-9677433-0-3

1. Educators. 2. Educational change.
3. Educational innovations. 4. Entrepreneurship
5. Education — Aims and objectives. I. Lavaroni, Charles. II. Title.

LB885.L452000 370.102'0922
QB100-252

10 9 8 7 6 5 4 3 2 1

We dedicate this book to Mrs. Joan Strawn, whose leadership assisted in making one of our entrepreneurial dreams a reality.

# Acknowledgments

Special thanks to our wives, Barbara and Pat, and our families, who encouraged and supported our efforts throughout the process of writing this book.

We extend our appreciation to Kristen Cauz, Barbara Dimmitt, Dr. Guilbert Hentschke, Ellen Kleiner, Laurie Lavaroni, Dr. John McLaughlin, Marie Schlossman, and Chris Yelich for their ideas, suggestions, and assistance in developing and writing this book.

We also acknowledge all the dedicated and marvelous teachers and administrators, in public and private schools, with whom we were fortunate to work throughout our careers.

We honor and celebrate all those educational entrepreneurs past, present, and future willing to risk their time, energy, and personal resources in creating products, programs, services, or technologies to improve learning for young people.

# Contents

# Foreword

Our image of schooling changes slowly but fundamentally over time. The one-room schoolhouse with its "school marm" was long ago eclipsed by the popular image of the massive urban public school, frayed at the edges from overuse and teeming with thousands of students and harried teachers. Just as no popular image is reflective of all, or even most, of reality at the time, each captures a central tendency, an essence of what many of us think of when we think about schools.

Our current images of public schools, whatever they may be, are inherently out of date. They are images of a familiar but recent past reality that is already being transformed in the present. A future popular image is already being created, even as we conjure up the present one. The one-room rural schoolhouse/classroom and the massive urban school portray not only older and more recent realities, but also concurrent realities with different histories.

Just as elements of the past remain as viable ingredients in the present, elements of the future state of schooling are already in evidence today. In contrast to the relatively isolated one-room school, today's large public school is also a local manifestation of a very large, complex school "system" composed of districts, states, and a densely woven web of governmental agencies and departments. Upon closer examination, our view of this largely governmentally controlled system is itself changing, in scope, scale, and economic organization. Today's complex, largely governmental education system is evolving into a global, multisector, rapidly growing and changing "service industry."

Of course, our local school districts with their (on average) six neighborhood schools continue to operate within traditional county, state, and federal structures. But growing up around this structure is a plethora of highly specialized for-profit and private nonprofit "education businesses" that provide services and goods that complement, supplement, and sometimes supplant the services traditionally provided by public school teachers. These businesses pursue market niches that include tutoring, technology training (for teachers as well as students), elementary science education, non-English language instruction, education-oriented child care, classroom materials, teacher staff development, special education, high school drop-out prevention, college advising, homeschooling services, and student travel programming. For-profit education businesses are even operating entire schools, These education businesses range in size from small (one person) enterprises to publicly traded, multinationals with workforces numbering in the tens of thousands.

Education, historically a social service, is now also becoming an industry, and a big one at that. Worldwide, it constitutes a $2 trillion business, of which over $700 billion operates within the US, about half of which is concentrated on elementary and secondary schools. A small but rapidly growing share of this expanding business is generated by for-profit firms. The drivers of this growth are both broadly social (frustrated with low levels of reported student achievement) and intimately personal. For instance, the pay gap between individuals with a college education and those without has widened from 50 percent in 1980 to about 111 percent today. Heightened demands of the education system are, at the same time, opportunities for entrepreneurs to develop goods and services that address those demands. Schooling has become simultaneously a personal improvement strategy, a cornerstone for regional economic development, a national priority — and a business opportunity.

A global education industry is thus growing up around the "education system," which in turn grew up around the one-room school. But what about parallel changes in the kinds of people who are the educators? Schools, systems, and industries are, after all, really only agglomerations of people. It is the people in education who ultimately define the stereotype of education. Is the stereotypical teacher being gradually replaced by the stereotypical businessperson in today's education industry? Through the brief biographies of twenty-two educational entrepreneurs, Donald Leisey and Charles Lavaroni break down both stereotypes and paint a portrait of the new educator in the most rapidly growing part of the education industry — the educational entrepreneur.

*The Educational Entrepreneur* is in part a study of the transformation of schooling from a system to an industry and in part a study of the transformation of people — educators who largely started their adult work life as teachers in classrooms. Somewhere along the way they developed a sense of what is most important to them as educators and how developing a business appeared to be the most compelling way to pursue that passion.

Meet, for example, Beverly Stewart Cox. "The classroom was great – interacting all day with eight year olds is quite stimulating. But I felt as if I couldn't reach every child..., there would always be one or two who would slip through the cracks." Convinced that these children could learn if someone worked with them one-on-one, she had a vision of reaching as many of them as she could through her own tutoring service (Back to Basics Tutoring Service, Inc.).

Social studies teacher Randy Gaschler came to a different epiphany but in a similar manner. "I was stunned that there was so much difference of opinion out there about how children learn best. Everybody's approach worked for somebody, but it was obvious to me that nobody knew the best way. My next thought was that no one should be deciding which philosophy is tried on which kid except the parent, because if an approach doesn't work, the parent bears the brunt of it." His pathway led him to establish a network for homeschooling (Innovative Education Management).

Kindergarten teacher Kay Fredericks found that her bulletin boards had become the envy of the faculty. She created large colorful cutout figures and characters about two and a half feet high to cover the wall-to-wall bulletin boards in her classroom.

She did all of these because she believed that attractive and stimulating room environments were critically important ingredients for the students and there was nothing commercially available to her or her colleagues at the time. After repeated requests that she produce displays for her friends' classrooms, Kay turned her passion into a business (TREND enterprises, Inc.).

Educators who read *The Educational Entrepreneur* should proceed with caution. They could well encounter reflections of themselves among the pages. These twenty-two educators find themselves in all manner of teaching circumstances. They develop a sense of beliefs about teaching and learning that are at the core of their being. They encounter frustration with early teaching situations — from constraints on what they are permitted to do, coupled by a growing realization of what they are uniquely capable of doing. Finally, usually at some risk, they make the decision to convert their professional hobby and passion into their profession by forming a business. Their freedom to pursue their passion finds them working harder and, for these individuals, gaining the satisfaction that comes from creating a successful educational enterprise.

Much like the professional histories of the two authors, the career pathways of the educators portrayed in *The Educational Entrepreneur* serve both to illuminate and to inspire. They debunk the myths, prevalent among all too many educators, that for-profit businesses in education must be categorically distrusted, and that people in business can only be in it for the money. At the same time, the authors illuminate the possibilities within many other educators — the possibility of professional fulfillment and service through entrepreneurship in education.

*Dr. Guilbert C. Hentschke, Professor*
*University of Southern California*
*Rossier School of Education*

# Preface

Educational entrepreneur? It's a term we coined to describe our situation as educators who have moved on to establish educational businesses. We know the turf well. Between us, we have a combined ninety years' experience in education, both public and private. We began our careers in public schools, where we each served for many years in the capacity of classroom teacher, principal, assistant superintendent, and superintendent. Then we ventured forth as independent advocates of learning.

Why did we strike out on our own? Although we enjoyed many aspects of public education, particularly the opportunity to work with talented and dedicated educators, we became disenchanted with the use of the public education system as a "political football," which hampered teacher creativity and administrative effectiveness. We grew increasingly frustrated by the politicians using public schools to solve societal problems, which took away from the efforts to educate children. Instead of tending to the educational needs of children, we found ourselves steeped in implementing new legislation and mired in bureaucratic rules and regulations.

Although we knew each other professionally, we didn't really know what values we shared professionally until we met in 1979, shortly after the passage of Proposition 13, the California property tax initiative. It was at this meeting that educational sparks flew when we discovered we were looking for the same thing: autonomy. We wanted the freedom to set our own curriculum and reach individual children in the best way possible. Determined to move toward our goals, we decided to become business partners. In 1980, we purchased Kittredge School in San Francisco, and the following year Merryhill School in Sacramento. Both of these successful independent schools were established in the 1940s.

Our departure from the public sector became an epiphany. Windows opened. Doors unlatched. Ideas bred realities — as in the following scenario, which took place in 1980, before computers became common learning tools in public schools.

Don: "Chuck, I think we should begin a computer literacy program and purchase computers for the students at Kittredge."

Chuck: "How many should we purchase?"

Don: "Oh, eight or ten."

Chuck: "Great, let's get ten."

In less than a minute, we decided to add computer literacy to our curriculum — an enhancement that in public schools would take exhausting committee meetings and negotiations over a long period of time. We were elated, because we knew we were onto something. We could make quick and effective decisions, and improve the students' prospects for learning. In fact, we knew we had to make good educational decisions, because the parents of our students had numerous alternatives available to them for educating their children.

Our elation kept right on growing. Both Kittredge and Merryhill flourished. Chuck founded the National Independent Private Schools Association (NIPSA), which now is recognized and legitimized by the US Office of Education as an approved accrediting body of for-profit education. Don expanded Merryhill's program to spawn twenty-two schools throughout northern California, under the name of Merryhill Country Schools before it was sold to a NASDAQ company in 1989. He then created The Report Card, Inc., which operates educational resource stores and catalog and Internet sales.

Recently, we founded the International Academy for Educational Entrepreneurship (IAEE), which we currently codirect. The mission of IAEE is to identify, encourage, and support educators who have already invested or are interested in investing time, energy, and capital to create, develop, and market programs, products, services, and/or technologies designed to enhance and improve education.

Having met many like-minded men and women during our years as educators, we became convinced their stories needed to be told. This book, the Academy's first project, profiles a sampling of success stories about educational entrepreneurs. Its intent is to celebrate the experiences of people who have given up secure jobs to create their own businesses, with the goal of improving society through advances in education. We hope their stories will inspire you — whether you're a parent, an educator, a public official, or a businessperson — to take the risk and invent new and exciting learning delivery systems that will enhance and improve the education of our youth.

# Introduction

*The Educational Entrepreneur: Making a Difference* is a result of our deep appreciation and respect for the American free enterprise system, which allows and encourages individuals to become entrepreneurs. The book is an outgrowth of our professional experiences, commitment to quality education, and passion for lifelong learning. Our many years of experience dedicated to education have convinced us that changes must be made. For education of high quality to flourish, we believe that entrepreneurism in education is the key to identifying and implementing those changes.

We have been fortunate throughout our careers in both public and private education to have worked with many extremely talented, creative, and dedicated teachers and other professionals. We are convinced that for positive changes to take place in the field of education, the vast potential of outstanding educators must be allowed to fully develop and be properly rewarded. For it is these committed people who will take advantage of the exciting new opportunities to transform education.

As educators, we have been able to observe education from many perspectives by serving in leadership positions at every level of education, both public and private, including preschool, elementary school, middle or junior high school, high school, college, and graduate school. We have experienced the great American Dream — the joy and excitement that comes from creating an educational business. We have felt the fears and frustrations of uncertainty about financial security for our families and our businesses, and concern about whether we would be able to meet our payrolls, pay our bills, and service our loans.

Through being in business, we have learned the connection between autonomy and social responsibility. We have sensed the personal satisfaction and pride resulting from effort and sacrifice. We have enjoyed wonderful words of gratitude from parents and former students for the educational programs we provided in our schools.

In 1998, we established the International Academy for Educational Entrepreneurship (IAEE). The mission of IAEE is to identify, encourage, and support educators who have already invested or are interested in investing time, energy, and capital to create, develop, and market programs, products, services, and/or technologies designed to enhance and improve education. We decided IAEE's first endeavor should be a book profiling and celebrating successful educational entrepreneurs.

This book features twenty-two educational entrepreneurs representing a variety of educational businesses. Some of the businesses represented have international dealings. The businesses include for-profit and not-for-profit private schools; educational travel services; early childhood programs; developers, manufacturers, and publishers of educational products, and media; an author of children's books; tutorial services; a school for high-risk students; a homeschooling management network; educational consultants for curriculum and charter schools; an educational software publisher; an educational camp; and an educational retail company. The companies of these educational entrepreneurs range in size from small family businesses generating a few hundred thousand dollars in revenue each year to a company that recently sold for over $1 billion. Three of the individuals featured have sold their companies but continue to stay active in educational endeavors, and one passed away in January 2000.

The educational entrepreneurs were selected from individuals we already knew or who were recommended to us. These educational entrepreneurs established a variety of educational businesses that have had a dramatic impact on education. The profiles of educational entrepreneurs in this book have been gleaned from on-site and/or telephone interviews, articles, testimonials, books, information on the Internet, and other source materials that provide candid views of each individual. Prior to publication, those educational entrepreneurs featured reviewed their chapter for accuracy.

Of course, all the women and men featured in this book are unique individuals from different age groups, backgrounds, and socioeconomic situations. Likewise, they have had very different experiences as educational entrepreneurs. Many have found that their entrepreneurial efforts have solidified their marriages; a few just the opposite. Some have businesses that have been in existence for over twenty-five years; others for as little as five or six years. Most have actively participated in their businesses with their spouse and/or children. Many have had some false starts. Most, if not all, have watched their business transformed to meet changing needs. Most have found ways to work directly with both public and private institutions for the improvement of learning. Some of the businesses rely heavily on public contracts and funds. All truly enjoy and appreciate the freedom that comes from their own initiative, while a few admit they sometimes miss some of the "perks" that come from being an employee in a traditional school setting. Most find that long workdays and workweeks, though somewhat limiting, are very satisfying. Most see themselves as providing leadership, not only to their profession but also to their communities. While in all cases the monetary rewards have been enough to keep each business profitable, money has never been the major motivator for any of them. Collectively, these educational entrepreneurs provide a number of "life models" for others to consider as they make personal and professional decisions.

Never before in the history of American education has there been a period with more opportunities for educational entrepreneurship. In the United States over $700 billion is spent on education annually, of which approximately half is for grades kindergarten through twelve. This amount represents approximately 10 percent of the Gross Domestic Product, second only to health care. The estimated annual revenues of for-profit educational services are $70 billion and growing at a rate of 25 percent a year.

New markets are emerging each year. Educational programs, products, services, and technologies that were unheard of or merely discussed hypothetically ten years ago are now becoming reality. These include voucher programs, charter schools, homeschooling, virtual learning, distance learning, and various software programs. In addition, the current high demand for more private schools, tutorial services, preschool education, child care programs, programs for high-risk students, and many other educational programs, products, services, and technologies prove that parents are willing to pay for better and more flexible education over and above their tax dollars.

*Webster's Dictionary* defines an entrepreneur as, "A person who organizes and manages an enterprise, especially a business, usually with considerable initiative and risk." For the purpose of this book, an educational entrepreneur is an individual who has served as an educator prior to organizing a business related to education and has invested time, energy, and capital to create, develop, and market a program, product, service, or technology designed to enhance and improve learning. It is important to note that according to this definition, educators who left the profession as entrepreneurs in fields unrelated to education do not qualify. Nor do the many educators who went to work for corporations and businesses, even though those businesses may be directly related to education. The educational entrepreneurs profiled in this book used their own resources to start and maintain a new venture — an initiative that puts them in a class by themselves.

After reflecting on the experiences of the educational entrepreneurs featured in this book and the literature on entrepreneurship, we have found the following qualities to be attributes of educational entrepreneurs: tenacious, optimistic, creative, courageous, persistent, willing to take risks, resourceful, independent, opportunistic, and thoughtful.

The educational entrepreneurs featured in this book are educators who personify these attributes. They have turned their dreams into innumerable benefits to the field of education. They have taken ordinary educational concepts and made them extraordinary. They have a refreshing passion for education and a tireless dedication to making a difference in the lives of children. They recognize the need for alternative delivery systems to meet the various learning styles of students. They dare to be a different kind of educator, primarily motivated by a strong desire to improve learning. They have given up the security of tenure, retirement systems, automatic pay increases, long summer recesses, and many other benefits of the teaching profession to contribute something of unique value to education and to find self-fulfillment.

These educational entrepreneurs are adventurous risk-takers who were not afraid to put everything on the line. Where others see problems, these educators see opportunities. They began their businesses with little more than a good idea and a strong determination to make the idea work. To finance the establishment of their businesses, these individuals withdrew retirement funds; took out second mortgages on their houses; spent their children's educational funds; borrowed money from banks, relatives, or friends; and employed other forms of creative financing. Generally, they kept their "day jobs" while testing the waters of educational entrepreneurism by working on their new business ventures in the evenings, weekends, or during summer recesses. After they were able to eke out a living from their new ventures, they plunged into their businesses full-time, successfully growing them.

As we focused on the lives of these educational entrepreneurs who are making a difference, we found two important common threads. First, these educational entrepreneurs do not ask the question, "How can I improve schools?" Instead, they ask, "How can I improve education and learning?" They have found the first question too limiting. The second question, by focusing on processes, opens up many new ideas, possibilities, concepts, applications of human resources, uses of technology, procedures for delivering instruction, and structures for organizing delivery systems.

Second, none of these educational entrepreneurs changed their goals; they merely altered the strategies they employed in achieving them. Without exception, these entrepreneurs chose education as their profession, and their goal was to improve the lives of children and the well-being of society. They did that as educators and they are continuing to do that as educational entrepreneurs. They still make a difference, but today they are doing it in more innovative ways and for more people.

There are certainly many educators who wish to become more independent, creative, and take greater responsibility for their lives. Over the years, we have been approached on numerous occasions by educators who were interested in how they could organize a business around an educational idea. Although this is not necessarily a how-to book, we hope educators who are considering going into business will obtain useful information from the various models provided by reflecting upon these educational entrepreneurs in relation to their own lives.

Not only educators will find these educational entrepreneurs of interest. Business leaders, elected officials, and the general public who see education as something more than buildings, books, and schedules will find the lives of these educational entrepreneurs compelling. For it is through such individuals that new ideas will emerge and improvements and innovations will be made to enhance the educational process. In the future, we envision the focus shifting from schools to learning so that questions like "How do we improve learning?" will replace the confining and limited "How do we improve schools?" And there will be more emphasis on exciting new possibilities in education, rather than criticism of current problems. We believe that the necessary changes in education will be provided in the future by educational entrepreneurs.

We consider it an extreme privilege to get to know the outstanding individuals profiled in this book, and to honor and celebrate their successful endeavors. These educational entrepreneurs have earned our deepest gratitude and admiration, and we hope they will inspire others to find their own creative methods of improving learning and education.

# Chapter 1

## Embracing Challenge

### Challenger Schools

*Inspiring children to embrace challenge and find joy and self-worth through achievement*

**Barbara B. Baker, Founder**

For the past several years, parents who wanted to enroll their preschool or kindergarten children in one of the very popular Challenger Schools located in Silicon Valley around San Jose, California, have found ingenious ways of making that possible. Many have camped in tents for days before the office opened for registration. They all wanted their children to have an educational experience that would launch them on a course of lifelong learning. Since it was established in 1963, Challenger has had the reputation of meeting that formidable task — a reputation that has helped Challenger grow from a one-room school of six preschool students to a total of seventeen locations, eleven in California and six in Utah, with corporate offices in Campbell, California, and Sandy, Utah. Collectively these schools, which are accredited by the National Independent Private Schools Association (NIPSA), serve over 7,500 students.

The fact that Challenger Schools have been successfully operating for thirty-seven years certainly proves that Barbara

Baker's vision of what an exciting education program could do for students was valid.

## Window of Opportunity

By the time Challenger was founded, Baker had already had several experiences in education. She had earned her BS and elementary teaching credential from Brigham Young University, and later her MEd in psychology, counseling, and guidance, again from BYU. She had also taught primary grades in the public schools.

Her disheartening experience while teaching the first grade was a prime motivating factor in establishing Challenger. Baker felt that children came to her from kindergarten functioning far below their capabilities and badly needed better training. She recalls, "The focus of kindergarten was all social. It seemed to me that the kindergarten experience had been wasted. By the time they were six years old, the children had already passed their prime learning era. I wanted to teach them at the most important time of their life. I wanted to focus on their excitement, their curiosity, and their joy for learning. As the public schools were constituted, I knew I could not do that in the way that made sense to me. The power of phonics was not only ignored, it was ridiculed. So I decided to start a preschool, one that would focus on the kinds of learning experiences I believed would provide a foundation leading to success."

Countless studies confirm what Baker knew from experience, observation, and intuition about the nature of childhood cognitive development. The window of opportunity for laying the crucial bedrock of cognitive skills and knowledge is brief and extends from infancy through age nine, as established by neuroscience. Therefore, the ideal time for children to learn phonics and develop the foundation for important cognitive skills is when their learning speed is at its peak in preschool.

As a result, Baker made her courageous and inspired decision to establish Challenger in 1963. Her vision was timely, and the programs innovative. Describing the characteristics and goals of the first Challenger School, she states, "I began Challenger Preschool in San Jose, California. I had a total of six paying students in a small remodeled house that my husband and I had purchased as an investment. The name Challenger was chosen because at the very base of any learning is the excitement that comes with that learning. I knew that excitement can best be created by small, incremental, recognizable, and attainable learning challenges. My basic curriculum was phonics and foundational academic skills taught with lots of music, action, and humor. I found that children, excited to learn what a cow says, are just as excited to learn that a '*b* says buh.'

"My students gained a foundation that could never be taken away from them. The preschool was a pleasant mix of music, academic foundation, art, play, drama, science, and physical activity. From the very first, we emphasized personal responsibility and respect for the rights of others. It must have been exactly the right time for this kind of education in the Santa Clara Valley, for the school grew from six students to one hundred in the first year. By the third year, with a waiting list of one hundred, we opened our first four-room preschool."

### Preparation for Self-Reliance

Today, Challenger's mission statement reflects the vision that motivated Baker to establish the first program. Baker says, "Our mission is to prepare children to become self-reliant, productive individuals; to teach them to think, speak, and write with clarity, precision, and independence; and to inspire them to embrace challenge and find joy and self-worth through achievement."

As Challenger expands, many constants remain, such as Baker's vision reflected in the mission statement and the manner in which each school is established and operated. Every school starts with a preschool and kindergarten program. During the following years, elementary grade levels are added. Today, out of the seventeen schools, three California schools are set up to meet the educational needs and interests of students from preschool through eighth grade. One school in Sandy, Utah, serves students from the first through the eighth grades. The others range from preschool–kindergarten (P–K), to the sixth grade.

Elementary school teachers are selected in a unique way. Every candidate must take a three- to four-hour test developed by Baker and the staff, one which requires the candidate to perform the types of tasks expected by Challenger graduates. In a difficult language section, the candidate is given something to read and then asked to answer questions and write an essay discussing the text. Baker has found that there is very little correlation in test scores between credentialed candidates and those who have not completed a credential program. And because Challenger is an independent school, teachers can be hired without state teaching credentials. So, while most Challenger elementary teachers have degrees, about 50 percent do not have a teaching credential. Moreover, Challenger has very high standards for prospective teachers. Says Baker, "Sometimes we go through upwards of fifty candidates before we find one we think has the qualities we want to see and reinforce in our schools."

Training for Challenger preschool and elementary teachers is equally thorough. There is a week-long training designed to ensure that every staff member not only understands the Challenger philosophy but is proficient in translating it into an exciting instructional program. During the first year, every teacher is assigned a mentor who is a teacher with at least two years' experience in the Challenger system. The second year for the new teacher is considered a practice year. By completing the requirements of the Challenger certification program, in the third year the successful teacher becomes a mentor. After three years of certification, the teacher becomes a master teacher and is awarded a silver medallion. Finally, after the fourth year of the program the teacher receives a master gold medallion.

Some other constants are: Students are required to wear uniforms; teachers are free to tutor individual students as their clients; extended day opportunities for students, from 7:00 to 8:30 A.M. and 3:30 to 6:00 P.M., are provided at every site; extra afterschool activities in such subjects as karate, piano, and French are offered at most locations; and there is an administrator at each location to ensure the constant application of the Challenger philosophy. Fortunately, in spite of phenomenal growth, the elements that have made Challenger special remain, although Baker is aware of how difficult it might be to maintain them in the future. According to her, independence and innovation are responsible for Challenger's continued success: "I am aware of and truly appreciate how much freedom I enjoy in this country of ours. My school is dependent entirely upon the success of our program. We receive no government money. That's why I am wary of vouchers. I think that if we accepted vouchers, we would be increasingly required to incorporate policies that are not compatible with our own. I think parents should have choice and control, and for that reason I like tax credits as opposed to vouchers."

## Payoff of Persistence

Baker says, "Challenger is more than a school; it is a philosophy." The same might be said of all excellent schools. Schools that cannot translate a distinct philosophy into recognizable and viable programs do not rise to such a level. While many outstanding schools reflect the visions of their individual leaders, Challenger is unique in that an aggregation of seventeen schools exhibit a uniform image, program, and philosophy. Such an accomplishment reflects the commitment and diligence of all staff. When asked about the secret of Challenger's success, Baker remarks, "If anybody were to ask me what it took to do what we've done, I would say 'persistence.' That is the key to life and success. You can be educated. You can have lots of money. You can be talented and bright. But without persistence, long-term success does not happen. You also have to know how to find the people who can help. You have to be able to trust them, to allow them to grow. Part of the success of Challenger comes from the constant application of our vision. I find that people will succeed if you let them know what the challenges are, have faith in them, allow them the right to fail and succeed, and give them the support to succeed."

Despite Baker's success and satisfaction, she has also experienced pain and made sacrifices during her years as an entrepreneur. Challenger was the result of a joint effort with her husband. Unfortunately, growing the business created some conflicts in their marriage. Baker remembers, "I was very happy with what I was doing and wanted to take Challenger to as many children as possible. He wanted to do other things, so in 1985 I bought his stock. It was good that he could go his way and I could go mine." Other members of Baker's family have enjoyed being part of the business. Five of Baker's six children have been active participants in the corporation. And currently one of her sons is its CEO.

A visitor to a Challenger School is impressed by the variety of activities and the high regard in which students are held. Student writings are abundant. There is always evidence of student participation in academic contests such as spelling bees, geography bees, math contests, and poetry competitions. Individual students are recognized and honored. In addition, the school's atmosphere is upbeat with the joyful sounds of music heard throughout the school. Since Challenger's beginnings, music has been important to the curriculum. Music is both a subject of every grade and an essential means of delivering content. Melody and rhythm are intertwined with nearly every subject. Preschoolers sing about science, elementary classrooms ring out with spelling chants, and middle school students rap about arithmetic. Some of the learning songs, chants, and drills were originally developed by Baker herself and have been in use for years. Others were written by talented and creative staff members. Creating such musical learning activities is one requirement of the Challenger certification process.

Baker's early experience with music helped shape her notions about success and commitment. She says, "My mother insisted that I take piano lessons at the age of eight. Not only did I learn piano, but it was music that proved to me the benefits of persistence. I would complain about practicing, and she would let me know I was going to practice whether I liked it or not. I not only learned to play music, but also found that it was fun and easy to compose music for children."

Baker is a firm believer in the power of music as a means to improve learning, creativity, self-image, and classroom discipline. She also maintains that music enriches life generally: "Giving students lifelong appreciation of music is reason enough to include it in the curriculum. People's reluctance to sing in social situations is quite noticeable today. I think it is sad that a whole part of the enjoyment of life is missing for so many people. I believe that the Challenger family will not have that void. In fact, we have even provided a simple and yet effective five-part suggestion list to all parents, entitled 'Harmony at Home: What Parents Can Do.' This list is designed to help parents use music to sharpen their children's minds as well as to enjoy their lives together."

Like many other educational entrepreneurs, Baker has added products, programs, and services to the basic business. A separate corporation, The Learning Crew, produces a colorful and exciting video program for preschool children ages one to seven, entitled *Challenger Phonics Fun,* which is based on the successful Challenger School phonics program. This program makes it possible for children who are not able to attend a Challenger School to still experience such education in "small, incremental, recognizable, attainable learning challenges." Moreover, the videos, cards, prereaders, as well as parent's suggestion books produced by the corporation are typically infused with music, fun, and activity. Thus, Baker has also made it possible for people at home to experience some of the unique features of a Challenger School.

# Chapter 2

## Marketing Mediation

### Ombudsman Educational Services

*Alternative education programs for at-risk youth*

**James P. "Jim" Boyle, Founder**

A newspaper article written in the December 4, 1982 issue of *The News-Sun* of Lake County, Illinois, entitled "Alternative Education: Man of Ideas," aptly describes James Boyle and his many years of entrepreneurial efforts on behalf of education. In addition, his company, Ombudsman Educational Services, established to help young people, has been featured in such other publications as *The Miami Herald, The Baltimore Sun, USA Today, The Chicago Tribune,* and *Forbes Magazine.*

Today, Ombudsman Educational Services has over seventy storefront programs in eleven states, serving over 3,000 students. A great majority of these students come from high schools while a few are of middle school age. And on rare occasions, nineteen- to twenty-year-old dropouts are admitted to the program.

The program is supported by the local school district. The uncomplicated one-page contract between Ombudsman and the district describes each party's responsibility. In essence, Ombudsman provides an individualized learning program for each student, continuous progress reports, and all required attendance and test results to the student, the family, and the district. The district pays Ombudsman a fee per student significantly lower than the costs for students who remain in a regular program regardless of the state or district in which the program is located.

Students are often sent to the Ombudsman program as a last resort before expulsion. While many students are there for remedial work, Boyle reports that increasingly students who are disinterested and lack commitment are also admitted. He explains, "We are getting a lot of really bright, bored, and turned-off kids — a new category of the 'at risk' population. When a student is admitted, which is pretty much automatic upon the request of the district, the student is immediately made aware of the urgency of the situation. We explain that this is your last shot. This is your job. You must be here every day and on time. We expect you to do something while you are here. We are not baby-sitting you. You don't interfere in the learning of others. You get along with your fellow students and teachers. If you do drugs, alcohol, or gang stuff, you're out of here. You're history."

As a result of the clear expectations and substance of the program, its success rate is quite impressive, with retention averaging over 85 percent. Many students return to their district to graduate with their class with the district diploma, some receive their diploma directly from the program, and still others earn their GED. Ombudsman programs have been accredited by the North Central Association (NCA), after visitations by the NCA in Illinois, Indiana, Minnesota, and Arizona. Programs exist as far east as New Hampshire and as far west as Colorado. States with Ombudsman programs include Florida, Ohio, Indiana, Missouri, Kansas, and Texas.

Boyle graduated in 1957 from the University of Iowa with a major in marketing from the College of Commerce. About the end of his junior year he was informed he needed a minor, and someone told him that education was "easy." So Boyle took the necessary course work, did some student teaching, and earned a teaching certificate. Armed with a degree, a teaching credential, and a new, if only modest, interest in teaching, he thought he would try it for a year.

That year resulted in a significant change in Boyle's ideas concerning his priorities. It was during that year, while teaching drivers training, typing, and general business in Libertyville, Illinois, that Boyle began formulating a solid and recognizable philosophy about education. That philosophy, still espoused by him, was based on a fundamental belief in the spirit of young people, the excitement of new ideas, the integral relationships between self-esteem and positive learning, the recognition of how each individual learns differently, and the potential of every person. These ideas were the result of observation, reflection, and immense curiosity. They developed as Boyle paid attention not only to the successes of people and programs around him but to failures as well.

During the following sixteen years working in the public schools, Boyle assumed many different responsibilities that helped change his focus. He stopped teaching in the business department and in drivers training. Instead, he taught sociology and then psychology, eventually becoming principal and finally assistant superintendent.

## Providing Motivation and Opportunity

During Boyle's career at the high school, he and the staff developed innovative programs. At one point, a group of educators was invited to evaluate these programs, and among them was a college professor who said, "You know, many kids need an intermediary, someone who will stand between the kid and the bureaucracy. An ombudsman." The idea and the name struck a chord with Boyle.

Armed with a philosophy of education, a sense of confidence, a strong belief in changes necessary for education to thrive, and facing a very difficult employment situation, Boyle made a dramatic career change. As with other entrepreneurs, dissatisfaction was the catalyst that prompted his reassessment. Boyle says of that time: "I was working for a superintendent I just could not respect. I couldn't stay. I thought he was a jerk. So I decided to become an educational consultant, which by definition is an unemployed administrator. In 1973, at the age of forty, I made a pretty dramatic career change. I took out my retirement fund of about 15,000 dollars and began a new phase of my life. Fortunately, I had made some friends in neighboring districts and throughout Illinois. I began getting contracts to help with special projects and with specific problems. I wasn't getting rich, but I was making a living and, most importantly, learning a great deal."

In the 1960s and early 1970s there was increasing pressure from the US government, various state departments of education, and universities to develop plans to identify and help a range of student populations who were not experiencing success in the schools. As a result, Boyle began getting consulting contracts with districts that were focusing on this problem. In the process of working with these districts, he was able to translate his philosophy of education into a specific program that would meet these students' needs.

In 1975, Ombudsman Educational Services received its first contract to provide instruction to students in the North Chicago School District — a district that had been identified by the Children's Defense Fund of Washington, DC, as having one of the highest suspension and expulsion rates in the country. The superintendent knew he had to establish an alternative education program to meet the needs of these students. And since he was not interested in creating an alternative program himself, he asked Boyle to develop one for the district's at-risk and potential dropout high school students.

Subsequently, Boyle established the first Ombudsman program, aided by his previous experiences as a teacher, administrator, and consultant. In developing it, he placed great emphasis on the fact that each individual learns differently. He recalls, "I always knew that kids learned individually. So the first thing I had to do was develop a program that was individualized. We set up a curriculum based on specific learning competencies. In the process we developed a catalog of competencies, the majority of which focused on the basic skills of reading, language arts, and mathematics. Others were established to make sure students were learning concepts and skills from science, social science, life-management, as well as health and recreation. It was through this last set of competencies that we were able to meet the Illinois requirement for physical education. These competencies have been reviewed, evaluated, and rewritten several times since 1975, and they serve as the basis for our current successful individualized program. The refinements found in our program today reflect an ever-increasing use of computers, which we introduced into our program in 1979. Computers allowed us to add course ware from commercial sources, utilize better assessment tools, and introduce and maintain a more comprehensive record-keeping and communication program. While much has changed, our philosophy has remained the same. Every child can learn and will learn individually. Every student needs a structure that respects this individuality. Every student must have a clear-cut understanding of expectations and of responsibilities to the teacher and fellow students. Toward this end, every student signs a contract that clearly describes and outlines the work as well as the social behaviors required to remain in the program."

Boyle believes that it is the mission of Ombudsman to provide a real alternative for students who are experiencing significant difficulties in conventional schools. Ombudsman does this by offering a program that is both valuable and achievable for every student enrolled. He explains, "Within that perspective, the function of the educational process is to identify each student's needs and abilities, and provide both the motivation and opportunity to gain a sound education."

## Coordinating the Needs of Students

The initial 1975 program, which served twenty-five students at North Chicago High School, was evaluated and judged successful by the Illinois Office of Education. By 1978, Boyle had established eight centers throughout Illinois. Word of mouth continues to be the best marketing strategy for Ombudsman. The success of this strategy can be measured by the dramatic increase in the number of students served since its inception.

One element that has made Ombudsman so popular is that it is both separate from and connected with the district and school of attendance for which the service is provided. Each referring school district determines its course requirements, as well as the number of credits to be allowed for graduation from the student's home school, which is one of the desired results of the Ombudsman program. Ombudsman has the responsibility to coordinate student needs with the standards of the district. The district identifies what is expected, and Ombudsman provides the program that will allow the student to meet those expectations. This information all becomes part of the student's Individualized Learning Plan. While in the program, the student remains on the district's attendance rolls. Moreover, it is usually the district that issues the credits and, upon successful completion of the requirements, a diploma. However, with the approval of the district, Ombudsman may also grant graduation status for age-appropriate and credit-deficient students.

This cooperative relationship between districts and Ombudsman is understandably one of the reasons behind the success of the program. Today it is doing between $10 and $11 million of business each school year. Even so, it remains a very personal business. As Boyle points out, "It is still basically a mom-and-pop operation."

Although Ombudsman is not a charter school, it is very much like one. In Boyle's words, "We were a charter school before there were charter schools." Actually there are both similarities and differences between Ombudsman and charter schools. Some similarities are that both provide an alternative program for certain students, do not always have to follow the precise guidelines as do traditional schools, and are financed by school district funds. The differences are that whereas charter schools often receive the same amount of money per student as regular schools, Ombudsman receives less than the per-pupil costs of the district; charter schools are under direct control of the local district and/or state board of education, which is not the case at Ombudsman, an independent business; and while charter schools are tax free, Ombudsman is a tax-paying corporation.

Boyle is fascinated with the ideas generated by educational entrepreneurship. He finds thinking about how to improve education an exhilarating exercise. More importantly, he has found that providing a program that improves learning for a significant number of students is extremely rewarding. His advice to others contemplating risking time, energy, and money to realize their visions is straightforward. Boyle remarks, "You have to bring something to the marketplace that isn't there, or improve on what is there. We never tell schools we do a better job than they do. We just do it differently. We have a specific clientele. We have fewer restrictions. I think much of our success is built on the notion of supply and demand, much like any other business service or product. I know of entrepreneurs who went into the charter school movement, and the first thing they wanted to do was eliminate administration. So they eliminated the people, but that didn't eliminate the functions. As a result, some schools are going down the drain just because of poor administration."

In addition to sharing his vision, Boyle stresses that whether we are creating a new service, a new educational product, or a new program, we are going to have to sell it. To sell it we have to market it, and to create a structure to market it we must recognize that we are in the world of business. While Boyle's classroom experience taught him about learning, his administration experience taught him more about how to manage time and money. He feels strongly that without conscious effort to combine education with business, the entrepreneur is doomed to failure. Boyle states, "Unless you have broad experience, either directly or indirectly, plus a very recognizable product to offer, I would say you'd better stay where you are. It's a tough market — it always has been and will continue to be. But the challenge is exciting, and the possibilities for personal growth and satisfaction can be worth the effort even if you should fail. As any educator will say, you learn from your mistakes. An entrepreneur will tell you that you can make those mistakes pay off."

# Chapter 3

## International Networking

### The International Educator
### The International Schools Training Institute
### TieCare International, Inc.

*A trio of services for the international educator*

**Forrest A. Broman, Founder**

Forrest Broman's commitment to quality international education is the foundation of all his work. During his career in international education, Broman recognized the need for keeping the worldwide community of American Overseas Schools and other international schools informed and in communication with one another, thus prompting him to establish a newspaper and an institute. How this occurred is inspirational to potential entrepreneurs.

Broman was headmaster of the American International School in Tel Aviv, Israel, from 1973 to 1991, when he moved to a similar position in Caracas, Venezuela. In 1985, Broman took a sabbatical leave from the school in Israel and, with the moral support of several people, borrowed $5,000 from his first wife to publish a newspaper called *The International Educator* (TIE).

Broman's vision was to publish a newspaper that would offer significant news about education throughout the world. He wanted it to have editorials that focused on issues of concern and conflict, photographs, announcements, articles from a variety of sources, and advertisements from people and companies offering services, programs, and products. The cornerstone of TIE was announcing available teaching and administrative positions throughout the world.

Broman succeeded in establishing such a newspaper and today, TIE is published five times a year, with one issue (usually May's) featuring a supplement devoted entirely to jobs. TIE also offers its subscribers the *Guide to Finding a Job Abroad,* which helps interested teachers and administrators find a job in one of the 800 international schools that hire teachers from America, Canada, and the United Kingdom.

TIE went online in September 1999 with an interactive site where vacancies can be changed weekly and candidates can register with the Résumé Bank. Subscriptions have doubled since then, and the site has over 1,000 visitors a day. Ads have grown by 38 percent.

In 1989, Broman established the Principals Training Center for International School Leadership. The PTC is administered out of the same office as TIE. PTC's mission is to provide "training programs and other professional services that meet the unique needs of current and future administrators in international schools." Students completing four components of the program are awarded a Certificate of International School Leadership.

This program, under the umbrella organization of the International Schools Training Institute, along with a sister program, Centers for International Teacher Education, offers teachers and administrators the opportunity to earn master's degrees, elementary and secondary teaching certificates, administrative certificates, as well as a doctorate in cooperation with Trenton State College, California State University at Northridge, and Boston University.

A third major program with which Broman is affiliated is TieCare International. He serves as CEO of this private company, which provides several insurance packages to the international school community. Through this company, located in Foothill Ranch, California, international schools and their staff can purchase most of their insurance needs, including health insurance, long-term disability insurance, and life insurance.

While working in all these capacities, Broman spends considerable time traveling throughout the world. Currently his home is in Caracas, Venezuela, while his offices are in Massachusetts and California. The people he serves are located in practically every country in the world, including the Balkans, China, and Pakistan. However, while one might envy his air reward miles, it would be difficult to covet his schedule.

## Standing Up for Beliefs

Broman's accomplishments are a result of his varied background. He has earned two degrees — a bachelor's in political science from Brown University, where he was Phi Beta Kappa, and a Doctor of Jurisprudence from Harvard Law School, where he graduated cum laude. After leaving Harvard, he first clerked in the Massachusetts Supreme Court and later joined a firm on Wall Street. From there, he went to work as an acting regional director in New York for the federal Anti-Poverty Program, which he refers to as "the war on poverty which turned out to be a skirmish." Next, he became a deputy commissioner for Mayor John Lindsay, with the responsibility for identifying talent for various appointments made by Lindsay.

Broman's experiences teaching overseas in many countries were pivotal to the establishment of his newspaper and institute. In tracing his move from New York to the world scene, he says: "When I was about thirty, I got a fellowship from something called the National Program for Educational Leadership. This program had as its goal the recruiting of people out of education into education. It was a nondegree program that was set up to bring a new kind of leadership to the schools. I taught in Harlem in a middle school, worked as a kindergarten teacher for a period of time in Long Island, and worked with a principal in White Plains. I became the first fellow in this program to go overseas. My overseas position was as an intern administrator in the American School of Israel. After a year the superintendent left, and I had the nerve to apply for his position, and I got it. I think I was the first intern to become a superintendent. This got me started in my international education career. I was in Tel Aviv for eighteen years. They were great years."

Broman feels strongly that his time in Israel had a profound effect on his life, and provided the foundation for his entrepreneurial efforts. While comparing the way things are done in America and Israel, he recognizes significant differences. To him Israel is a very direct, honest, open, blunt, almost confrontational kind of society, and to be effective in Israel it is necessary to be more assertive than in the United States. He feels his experiences made him stronger, more willing to take risks, and more adamant about standing up for his ideas. "I became more outspoken, much less embarrassed about my ideas and goals. I think that experience changed my personality. I became more willing to push my ideas and stand up for what I believe."

### Information for Mobility

Publishing the first issue of *The International Educator* was the turning point in his career. That first issue had twenty pages of news about topics of interest to international schools. It contained twenty-four ads that helped pay for printing, mailing, and other expenses. TIE was successful from the beginning and expanded quickly. During the first three years, the number of copies printed increased by several thousand. At that time, Broman was able to produce the publication himself since the school in Israel was well organized and had an excellent staff.

Originally, Broman established TIE as a nonprofit business to avoid potential conflicts of interest. Thus it was only later that Broman received compensation. He explains: "TIE is incorporated under a private, nonprofit corporation, the Overseas Schools Assistance Corporation (OSAC). Quite honestly, the reason we did this is because I had to flog this newspaper and the advertisements to guys I knew, to friends of mine. I felt more comfortable doing it for a nonprofit group. I didn't take a salary while I was headmaster, because I already had that salary. I did take expenses for travel. When people asked why I did that, I told them I knew that someday I would be in semiretirement and I'd collect then. That is exactly what has happened, and I do get paid very well now."

Today TIE, published in the range of 16,000 copies an issue, has well over 300 schools and companies as advertisers. A large number of universities, colleges, and public libraries are among its subscribers, including the Department of Defense Schools worldwide. TIE continues to provide important news and information useful to educators searching for employment. Broman estimates that in any given year about 4,000 to 5,000 available jobs are listed. As the executive director, Broman has the assistance of five full-time employees in the Cummaquid, Massachusetts, office; several part-time people; and individuals who sell ads and subscriptions for a commission. TIE is read by teachers, administrators, and school board members in every continent of the world except Antarctica. It is considered by many individuals and sectors of governments, including the United States, as one of the most important tools for communication in the international schools community.

In addition to establishing better communication between many overseas schools, Broman began a training program for administrators. Earlier, he was asked to write training grants for the Overseas School Advisory Council, a private group of people sponsored by the US State Department. It is made up of several corporate donors who provide funds to groups and individuals with ideas, programs, or services designed to positively influence American overseas schools. Since Broman had previous experience developing training materials and films for the State Department, he was in a good position to receive a large grant for the establishment of a principals training program. The first session, held in Rome, had twenty-eight people in attendance.

That first training session laid the foundation for the Principals Training Center, which since 1989 has trained over 2,500 administrators and teachers for service in overseas schools. People who successfully complete a series of four courses are awarded a certificate. Because of the success of the first series of courses, a second set of four courses leading to an advanced certificate was later added. Early on, Trenton State College, now the College of New Jersey, recognized the quality of instruction offered by the center when it allowed students to earn three graduate credits by adding a paper to the practical activities presented in the set of courses the center offered.

Broman envisioned the Principals Training Center programs as a means for providing strong principals to the international schools community. He says, "You really don't have change, improvement in instruction, or a strong environment for learning if you don't have a strong principal. It became increasingly clear to me and others that overseas schools were particularly vulnerable to that weakness. Often, principals came up through the ranks of counselor, as a popular teacher, or department head. When they returned to the States for work in administration, it was frequently irrelevant. US training programs were universally designed to prepare people for statewide public schools. The needs of principals working in independent overseas schools were significantly different. We wanted to create an institution that would provide the distinct kind of training and experience that an international school principal would need."

Today, the original concept of the Principals Training Center has been expanded to include the Center for Educational Teachers Education — a branch of the International Schools Training Institute (ISTI) that provides the liaison work making it possible for people to earn a variety of degrees or credentials from accredited American universities. ISTI is a for-profit corporation incorporated in the Bahamas since Broman hopes to eventually move his offices there. In the meantime, the corporate shares are owned and held by TIE.

Interestingly, ISTI is adding yet another program to its offerings — the Academy for International School Executives, which is designed to help headmasters and superintendents meet their responsibilities in this increasingly complex world. Broman says of this challenge: "They have no one to talk to. They are directly affected by wars, riots, and economic downturns. They are under constant scrutiny by demanding people who want high-quality private education even though they are in Timbuktu. There really isn't an institution that serves the personal and professional needs of these guys. We know we can help them and their boards. The Academy will operate as an independent institution with a board of interested school heads. We are helping create it as a way of thanking all those heads who have supported the PTC and TIE over the years."

As an entrepreneur establishing and growing a business, Broman knows the importance of providing a personnel benefit package that will encourage good people to seek employment with his companies and stay. Today, he not only has benefit packages for himself and his employees, but as the CEO of TieCare, he ensures that similar packages are available to many of the overseas schools. This development is a result of Broman's insight into the needs of overseas educators and the problems international schools face in addressing those needs. Broman knew from experience that overseas schools had difficulty in finding quality insurance programs for their staffs. Another entrepreneur who was interested in offering such programs knew of the excellent reputation of TIE. So in 1991, an agreement was reached for the use of the name. In 1998, Broman accepted the position of CEO to help strengthen the company and its continuing support of TIE's parent organization, OSAC. Commenting on this new role, he says: "It gave me another outreach to schools and another service that we could work on and perfect. So, since the summer of 1988, I have been an insurance executive. Who would have believed it?"

## Overcoming Entrepreneurial Inhibitions

When asked what advice Broman would give to someone thinking about becoming an educational entrepreneur, he has interesting counsel — some of which is practical and some philosophical. First he comments, "Don't give up your day job. Start small. Don't throw in all of your capital. Use part-time people to the extent you can. Put in as many extra hours as you can to build a foundation. Make sure that you can take some risks, even make some mistakes. Give yourself ten to fifteen years. Be ready to sacrifice."

To this he adds excellent observations about why a person might want to make such a decision: "I think most of us want to do more for ourselves. We want the freedom to be our own boss, to take more personal responsibility for our own efforts, and to get some monetary rewards at the same time we are receiving personal satisfaction. I know that was and is important to me. Also, always remember that whatever you do, it must have *quality*. It must bring you the emotional rewards that only an outstanding job can bring. If you can't be proud of what you do, then all the money in the world won't make it feel right. It won't bring you happiness."

Broman continues to have a keen interest in the future of international education and frequently considers new ways to improve it. He recognizes that he has learned a great deal about teaching and learning. He and his wife, Bambi, head of the Caracas school, feel a sense of commitment to the future. They are seriously considering taking the ideas they have learned in American schools overseas and helping the home countries use those ideas in their own native schools. As Broman explains: "Both Bambi and I feel strongly that our next role might be to work in countries that have really inferior schools. In some of these countries such schools are functioning almost next door to our schools. They are terrible. For example, they have no concept of making the school part of the community. They rely almost completely on rote memorization. It isn't just that they are poor; they have no idea what education is, what it can do for their country. We want to try to make a major contribution to improving some of those systems. That, right now, is the next thing on our agenda."

Finally, Broman offers some thoughts for our organization, the International Academy for Educational Entrepreneurship: "Go for it! I used to have lots of ideas but was afraid to act on them. I don't think I would have had the confidence to try if I hadn't gone to Israel. But we all can't go to Israel. The lesson for everybody today is that the world is rapidly changing. It is time to reach out, to try. It seems to me that the ideas the academy is putting forth have great potential, both for individuals and for the profession as a whole. Maybe they can help many new people get over the blocks, the fears, and the inhibitions that stand in the way of their realizing their goals and dreams. That would certainly be a valuable contribution to the future."

# Chapter 4

## Identifying Strategies for Success

### Search Models Unlimited
### The Institute for Intelligent Behavior

*Upgrading teaching and learning skills*

**Dr. Arthur L. Costa, Founder**

Many years ago, Art Costa made a promise to himself: he was going to devote his professional and personal life to the improvement of teaching and learning. At some point during that journey of professional development, he made a promise to his wife, Nancy: the Costas would someday live in Hawaii. Ultimately, it was possible to fulfill both promises.

Today, Costa's office is in his home in Kauai, overlooking the surf of the Pacific Ocean from high on a gentle, verdant slope. One room of the house is reserved for his entrepreneurial efforts, complete with telephone, fax, copy machine, and computers. This office makes it possible for Costa to continue his writing, workshop preparation, and correspondence with his many contacts throughout the world, as well as to communicate with his secretary and his travel agent on the mainland. Costa's secretary works with him in both of his complementary businesses. She serves as the coordinator for all of his speaking, workshop, and seminar responsibilities. She is the person with whom a potential client first makes contact when securing his service and knows where Costa is on any given day — not a particularly easy task as he is on the road for well over half the year.

Much of Costa's travel is in connection with his partnership with Dr. Bob Garmston at the Institute for Intelligent Behavior. This organization administers Costa and Garmston's copyrighted and service-marked program Cognitive Coaching, which helps teachers achieve a higher level of effectiveness in the classroom.

Costa's other company, Search Models Unlimited, administers and coordinates his other consulting and writing efforts. This sole-proprietorship presently has as its most important product his descriptions of behaviors that make up the attitudes and attributes of successful people. It is these behaviors, or "habits of the mind," that help teachers identify strategies students use when they do such things as solve problems, make decisions, self-evaluate, determine validity, and create.

## Developing "Cognitive Coaching"

From the first day Costa started teaching in southern California, he was fascinated with the processes people use to learn. As a seventh and eighth grade science teacher, he immediately saw the connection between the art of teaching and the science of teaching. Because of his success as a teacher and his enthusiasm as a learner, he was invited to join the Los Angeles County Superintendent of Schools Office as a science consultant.

In this position he further focused on the learning processes. He remarks: "I spent more time in front of teachers than kids. So I cut my teeth on becoming a consultant. Looking back, I know I made a lot of mistakes and fell on my face several times. But I got great support and encouragement from other people in that office. It was at this time that I began to develop my fascination with and understanding of how students learn in general and how teachers learn about teaching in particular."

After a few years with LA County, Costa joined NASA, becoming the director of Educational Programs for the eleven Western states. It was during this time that he met Dr. J. Richard Suchman, the originator of a fascinating teaching strategy, Inquiry Training. That meeting with Suchman, and their subsequent collaboration on the writing and the publication of a series of pamphlets on Inquiry Training, reinforced Costa's deepening interests in teaching and learning.

However, as time went on, Costa missed having a direct involvement in education, and subsequently, following a few years as an administrator in the Sacramento County Schools Office, began teaching again, this time at the university level. He describes his shift in perspective in the following way: "I was honored to be part of NASA's outreach program to educate the public about the social benefits that come with space travel and exploration. That was fun. I had access to materials and people who could make education exciting. But after a while I really missed contact with schools, kids, and teachers — and truthfully, working with the government was the pits. The people were great. The bureaucracy was horrible. After a time I realized I didn't want to do that anymore."

Costa's next job was assistant superintendent in the Sacramento County Office of Education. While working there, he managed to commute to the University of California at Berkeley, for night and Saturday classes, and eventually earn his PhD.

In 1970, California State University, Sacramento, invited Costa to join their Department of Education Administration and Supervision. Here he honed his teaching, writing, consulting, and presentation skills, and continued his exploration of teaching and learning even further. The position allowed him to grow so much he remained in it for twenty-two years. He says of these pivotal years: "That time was important to me. It gave me freedom. I really enjoyed teaching classes and working directly with students."

While still working at the university, Costa established his consulting firm, Search Models Unlimited. After the publication of an influential book he edited, his life changed dramatically. This occurred during a time of transformation in education. In his words: "There have been periods in history when cognitive education came to the forefront. In the 1960s, for example, we were faced with the Russian Sputnik. We were forced to think differently about education. People were hungry for something other than the old method of memorization. It happened again in the 1980s, when there was a push for critical thinking. The Association of Supervisor and Curriculum Development (ASCD) published a book I edited, *Developing Minds*. That book had a major influence on me. It was distributed to over 180,000 ASCD members overnight. The phones started ringing right away. I immediately became an independent consultant. I had to learn how to manage my responsibilities at the university with my emerging business. I had to hire a secretary. I had to create a separate entity, Search Models Unlimited, to keep my consulting business separate from my university work. I had to schedule many of my consultancies during the summer, on weekends, and between semesters. In hiring a secretary, purchasing my own equipment, setting up my own telephone line, and securing the services of an attorney, an accountant, and a graphic artist, I had become an entrepreneur. I had a business. I was not only thinking, I was doing."

Following his initial success, Costa continued his entrepreneurial efforts, but with a partner, Dr. Bob Garmston, who was also on the staff of the university. He and Garmston recognized their individual commitment to "developing a teacher evaluation program that was positive, helpful, constructive, trust building, and would promote self-evaluation." With this goal in mind, the coaching strategy "Cognitive Coaching" was launched, first as a part of the university program and later the foundation for the Institute for Intelligent Behavior (IIB).

Today, this institute trains people in the strategy designed to help develop the intellectual capacities of teachers. Twenty-five to thirty enthusiastic graduates of its leadership training program are authorized to conduct workshops in Cognitive Coaching — a name copyrighted by Costa and Garmston. Every time a workshop is offered, the Institute earns a royalty. In addition to the workshop materials that Costa and Garmston have published, their book has sold over 25,000 copies. The income from these combined sources makes IIB a financially successful business.

### Protecting Integrity

Costa admits that initially he and Garmston did not know how to go about marketing their product. "When we first started," he says, "it was just Bob and me doing it. We would go off and make a presentation. When the very first client asked how much time we needed, we looked at each other and said, 'Six days.' We got that figure out of the blue. We went to a conference ground and put on our first six-day workshop. We pretty much invented as we went along."

Now IIB has well-formulated policies, role definitions, and priorities designed to grow the business and protect the integrity of the product. It also has a manager who oversees the scheduling, the collection of royalties, and the storing and distribution of workshop materials, and who routes requests to the right people.

Costa is not as concerned with the growth of the company as he is with quality assurance. He notes, "Quality assurance is a real problem whenever you franchise or enlarge your circle of representatives." An important question for him has been: How do you ensure that a program stays consistent with the intent of the developers as they have less and less direct contact with it? This is a question that many entrepreneurs have to face, especially those who want to offer franchises. Some of the ways Costa and Garmston maintained quality are by offering a yearly symposium to help trainers upgrade their skills and knowledge; developing videotapes that model excellent coaching sessions; publishing a series of in-house newsletters; and constantly upgrading their Web site.

Costa has a clear sense of where he has been, where he is, and where he wants to go. Although he feels satisfied with his accomplishments, he remains concerned about improvements in education. And while the ideas and theories behind both "habits of the mind" and Cognitive Coaching have remained constant, their specific applications are constantly being refined and clarified. As Costa explains: "Conceptually they are the same. In other words, the beliefs, value system, and psychological principles have not changed. However, the delivery system and descriptions have been improved and will continue to be improved upon. The issue of keeping a product or program consistent and at the same time making improvements in it is an important one for all entrepreneurs to consider, especially those who try to bring change to the field of education."

Reflecting on the question "Isn't the balance between providing a quality product and at the same time improving upon it a problem facing all businesses?" Costa replies: "That's an interesting question. I'm not sure. What I am sure of is that we have a much clearer mission today than we did then. At first we merely wanted our products to be used in a given school or department. We don't want that anymore. Now we want to work with schools and districts that have interests similar to ours. We want to do more organizational change. We are interested in schools and districts that are on the cutting edge. We are looking at enhancing the intellectual processes of people. We want to work where our ideas can spread into the school as a whole, where curriculum, personnel practices, and staff development will be affected. Do all businesses go through that kind of metamorphosis? I really don't know." The two certainties for Costa and his businesses are *change* and *commitment to quality.*

## Remaining Open to Change

Predictably, Costa's advice to people interested in developing their own business focuses more on the issues of quality, commitment, and personal development than on profit, since for him the rewards have been more psychological than financial. Although he has done well and earned enough money to make his life more comfortable, his real satisfaction comes from people using ideas and concepts he has developed. Costa suggests several considerations a future educational entrepreneur should think about before establishing a business: "First of all, be sure you have something to sell that will be of value to someone. There has to be an audience or receiver for what you are selling. Also, while the ideas are important, they are meaningless unless they are presented well. For example, anyone who wants to become a presenter, workshop leader, or consultant must hone up on the requisite communication skills. Remember, the audience is not only listening but observing as well. The consultant is delivering many messages simultaneously. The process the consultant uses must be consistent with and supportive of the content of his message. Any consultant today must recognize that what he is offering has to support the big picture. He must think of the system as a whole. He also has to think of ways to make sure that his offerings will last on their own and are not dependent on him. He has to develop a delivery system that makes it possible for the program to grow and become institutionalized after he is no longer involved. Further, he has to be able to let go. Sometimes this is very difficult, especially when there is a question about how the program will be used, assessed, and evaluated."

According to Costa, although the integrity of a program or product is paramount, the integrity of the entrepreneur is of at least equal importance. Costa's message to entrepreneurs is direct and consistent with his beliefs and values: "You have to be a continuous learner. There is always a dimension in which you can improve your knowledge and skills. You have to continually refine, grow, test ideas, explore, try new ideas, and be open to the joys and frustrations of ongoing change. It is an attitude, if you will; a kind of humility. You know you don't know it all. Any time an entrepreneur thinks he's got it, he's reached the pinnacle—and that's the beginning of the end. If you ever achieve complacency and say, 'I've arrived,' watch out. You're probably on the decline."

# Chapter 5

## Emphasizing Educational Basics

### Back to Basics Tutoring Service, Inc.

*Tutoring programs for children and adults*

**Beverly Stewart Cox, Founder**

Most businesses mature slowly. But some go ballistic almost immediately, taking their founders on rides more exhilarating and exhausting than they had dared to expect. So it was for Beverly Stewart Cox, founder and president of Back to Basics Tutoring Service, Inc. The former third grade teacher, who started tutoring students in the kitchen of her one-bedroom apartment in 1985, now oversees a sprawling three-state operation based in Wilmington, Delaware.

"My vision was to educate as many people as I could, one-on-one," said Cox. But even she never anticipated being able to reach so many. By 1999, her company had some eighty employees and a fluctuating enrollment ranging from 350 in early fall to 500 in the spring, when students cram to get better report cards. Back to Basics Tutoring Service serves students from the pre-K level to adults in Delaware, Pennsylvania, and Maryland, offering year-round individual and small-group tutoring in more than fifty topics and providing customized services to corporations, hotels, restaurants, and school districts.

Despite its rapid expansion, this award-winning enterprise

still adheres to Cox's original twofold concept: emphasizing educational basics to lay the foundation for success in many areas, and creating an encouraging, positive atmosphere where learning is fun.

## Kitchen Tutoring

Cox gained the skills and knowledge she needed to conduct and supervise her tutoring operation well before she had the idea of starting one. She received a BA in elementary education and an MEd in special education from the University of Delaware, where she also took additional courses beyond the master's level that gave her expertise in psychology and testing. She then taught third grade at a Delaware private school for six years. There, the idealist in Cox confronted a reality she found difficult to accept — the disparity of learning among children.

"The classroom was great — interacting all day with eight year olds is quite stimulating. But I felt as if I couldn't reach every child. They all had different needs, backgrounds, and learning styles," Cox says. Convinced that all children could learn if someone worked with them individually, she had a vision of reaching as many of them as she could through her own tutoring service.

With determination, Cox decided to make a clean break from her "day job" and set about moonlighting at odd jobs to earn extra money during her last year of teaching. "As long as I could pay the basics like my rent and car payment each month, eat minimally, and buy some teaching supplies and business cards, I figured I was good to go," she remarks.

Asked what gave her the grit to fling herself headlong into an unproven solo venture, Cox credits her firm belief in what she wanted to attempt and the strong work ethic she had learned from her father. She also gained courage by sharing her enthusiasm with a friend who happened to be starting his own business at the time. Finally, Cox was further inspired by reading *Go for It*, by Irene Kassorla, and by attending a motivational three-day session of Tom Hopkins's Boot Camp in Scottsdale, Arizona.

Consequently in summer 1985, Cox rented a one-bedroom apartment on the ground floor of a duplex in Wilmington and gave notice that she would not be returning to teach school in

September. Equipped with a vision, a bankroll of $500 she had earned while moonlighting, a business license, some business cards, and eventually brochures, she dubbed her kitchen the "tutoring center" and set off in search of students.

To jump-start her business, Cox pounded the pavement day after day, visiting principals, headmasters, guidance counselors, psychologists, pediatricians, and other professionals who had contact with children. "I would give people a brief synopsis over the phone about the purpose of my intended visit, and I very rarely got turned down," she recalls.

Soon she had given out so many brochures that she had to order more. "Boy, when this hits, it's going to hit big," she confided to a friend. And she was right.

After a while Cox was working sixteen-hour days, seven days a week. She did the bookkeeping, promoted the business, tutored students, and worked to recruit more. Only four months after she had established the business, she hired a teacher as her first part-time employee. "I was tutoring in the kitchen, the parents were using the living room as a waiting room, and my employee was working in the dining room," Cox remarks.

Back to Basics Tutoring Service rocketed along, meeting all its one-year goals well ahead of schedule. The following year, Cox moved herself and the business into a nearby three-bedroom rental house and hired more employees. "Three years later, we were tutoring in every room except the bathroom," she jokes. And work done in the home office accounted for only a fraction of the business, since much of the tutoring was done off-site in deference to the needs of students.

In 1989, some luck and Cox's power of persuasion enabled her to convert a major challenge into a milestone. The business needed more space, and she found a commercial building for sale that was suitable for use as a tutoring center. But she ran into problems when she tried to apply for a loan. "The bankers basically laughed at me. They said, 'You are a female, you have been in business just over three years, and you are going to buy this three-story corner building with a garage in the city? I don't think so,' Cox remembers. Only one commercial banker was willing to listen. But after Cox showed him her bank accounts and other records documenting the company's growth, he told her she had not yet generated enough cash to make approval of a single loan likely. Nevertheless, the banker offered a solution to the dilemma: "He split the purchase into two loans and put them through separately. I never missed a loan payment. If it weren't for him, I wouldn't be in this building," Cox says.

Learning rapidly, Cox changed her enterprise from a sole proprietorship to a subchapter S corporation when she bought the building. Cox also gained the community support she needed to get approval for a zoning change. She even became a landlord for a while, renting out part of her new building to bring in extra cash until Back to Basics Tutoring Service, Inc. required the use of all three floors.

In 1990, Cox calculated that the company had posted an astonishing three-year growth rate of 123 percent. This kind of growth can sap the reserves of the most resilient entrepreneur, and Cox was no exception. Challenges in addition to keeping pace with her tutoring center's space requirements included the need to enhance benefit packages so she could attract and keep good employees, restructure staffing and programming periodically, and replace outgrown hardware and software. "When I come upon a new growing pain, it just stresses me out," Cox admits. "But it's wonderful on the other side of it, and I am better off."

Fortunately, Cox was blessed with phenomenal energy. Being single also gave her the freedom not to focus much on her personal life, especially in the beginning. "Any entrepreneur or dedicated businessperson will know that you eat, sleep, drink, and breathe the business. It never really gets easy. I still have those twelve- or sixteen-hour days sometimes. I eat at my desk; I haven't had more than twelve consecutive days off in fourteen years; and I rarely leave when I want to, because the phones are still ringing. But I eventually learned that if I wasn't careful, I would burn out. That was the last thing I wanted to do, because my work is such a passion to me. I want to do this for as long as I can, and I want to do it well," she says.

Avoiding burnout entailed hiring more office staff to free Cox from the urge to do everything herself. Not until 1997, however, did Cox make a move she advises others to make earlier if they can afford it: she hired a public relations person. "We advertised in local magazines and newspapers, and tried using billboards, but the bulk of our business has been word of mouth," she explains. "Our public relations person, who works for us part-time, has really gotten our name out. She has had articles published, done mock interviews with me, and even had me write informative articles about education, which allows me to give something back to the community in the form of answers to problems parents may have."

One thing Cox never did was enlist the aid of a partner or partners in the business. "That's a personal decision, but I would never consider it," she says. "I want to do things the way I think will be successful and right. Certainly I have made mistakes along the way, but I knew what I had to do and I needed to be the one to do it."

## Matching Methods to Needs

Having worked hard to establish her company's reputation, Cox remains committed to maintaining the highest standards. Her tutors are experienced professionals with degrees at the bachelor's, master's, or doctorate level. They are salaried or are paid by the hour as employees to maintain a clear relationship with the company.

Today, Cox herself rarely tutors, so she has had to develop new strategies for maintaining the "mom and pop" feeling of the company. "I perform quality checks of the tutors to be sure they are not just delivering basic professionalism but are bending over backwards to get results and communicate with the clients. My goal is to make sure we are achieving what we are paid for and expected to achieve," Cox emphasizes.

A glance at the brochure about Back to Basics Tutoring Service, Inc. reveals a program that is comprehensive, flexible, practical, and geared toward student success — whether for remedial or enrichment purposes. Individual tutoring is available for a wide range of topics including foreign languages, math, science, reading, English as a Second Language, study skills, keyboarding, public speaking, and achievement test preparation. The company also customizes programs for learning-disabled, hearing-impaired, homebound, and homeschooled students.

Back to Basics Tutoring Service, Inc. also has PhD level psychologists on staff to perform IQ and academic achievement testing. Results can be used to determine the need for special services provided by the schools or to document a student's eligibility to take untimed Scholastic Aptitude Tests. They also serve to illuminate students' particular strengths, weaknesses, and learning styles. Such results then enable tutors, parents, and other educators to match teaching methods to each student's needs.

Another hallmark of Cox's operation that distinguishes it from many other such ventures is its flexibility. Back to Basics Tutoring Service, Inc. is open seven days a week and is geared to take education to clients. While clients are free to come to the tutoring center, the bulk of the sessions are held wherever a student happens to be — at home, in the office, or at a daycare center, summer camp, or school. The logistics of running such a complex business in three states have been daunting, but by sticking with this approach, Cox has secured a special niche for her company.

"The tutors I hire live in various geographic areas, and they choose where they want to tutor," she explains. "Then, based on their degrees and their experience, they are set up with certain students for specific subjects."

## Enhancing Corporate Communication

Cox is quick and creative at responding to consumer-driven market opportunities. "I get bored easily, so I try to keep stimulating my own mind and challenging myself with new ventures," Cox confesses. "I won't go into arenas that I know nothing about, because that would take too long to research. But if I think I can hire someone or already have someone on my staff to do it, I will take on nearly anything we are asked to do."

Over the past ten years, Back to Basics Tutoring Service, Inc. has been providing services at the request of major corporations, such as DuPont, Hercules, and Marriott. Once, a construction company owner called to say he was having trouble with an employee who was wonderful at his job except that he had problems managing anger and would get huffy with some clients. The owner asked Cox to help this person improve his conflict resolution skills and professional demeanor. She had someone on staff who was perfect for this, and both employee and employer ended up satisfied.

Another opportunity for Back to Basics Tutoring Service, Inc. to provide service to corporations occurred naturally. "A Marriott hotel was holding periodic power meetings, and they asked if we could send people to interpret for several Spanish-speaking employees as well as two hearing-impaired employees. I said to myself, 'Sure, I have people I can tap into for that,' so I decided how much it was going to cost, called them back, and said I had it lined up," recalls Cox.

Today, Cox's company provides foreign language and sign language interpretation for international business meetings and social functions, as well as translation of company literature. For clients involved in international ventures, the personnel of Back to Basics Tutoring Service, Inc. teach technical math and sciences, English as a Second Language, and foreign language and cultural orientation. They also offer soft skill seminars on topics like time management, customer service, and diversity training. With an eye on the increasing globalization of the corporate sector, Cox observes, "I can only see expansion in this area."

Her newest endeavor involves sharing her vision and expertise with aspiring educational entrepreneurs — to help other people who are summoning the courage to be more innovative and independent. "I consult all over the country with people who are interested in setting up or growing their tutoring businesses, helping them to avoid pitfalls," Cox says.

So far, she has resisted franchising her business because of an unwillingness to lose control over quality or engage in "cranking out education like a production line." However, she sees her mentoring as a way of encouraging the spread of one-on-one education. "I didn't really have anyone I could talk to when I started in my early years, and I had to learn a lot as I went along. It's been tremendously rewarding to help others, and the fun part is that I'm still educating — not about math or English or spelling, but about starting and running a business," Cox adds.

As a result of her success, Cox has received numerous awards for her business acumen and her contribution to education. For example, she was named to the *Philadelphia Business Journal*'s Top 100 Companies in 1991, featured in *Entrepreneur Magazine* in 1995, nominated for the National Women of Enterprise Award in 1996 and 1997, and she won the 1998 Entrepreneurial Woman of the Year Award given by the New Castle County Chamber of Commerce and the *Delaware Capitol Review.*

These honors attest to Cox's mastery of corporate intricacies. But her advice to educators wondering if they, too, should leave their day job to start a business, sounds more visionary than tactical. "Some people are meant to be entrepreneurs, and some aren't," Cox states. "You have to know you can give your all. If you want your company to grow fairly large and be the sole source of your income, you are going to have to give up a lot. If you just want it to be part-time, that is a different story. Either way, if you provide quality service and try to meet every need you can, the rest will follow."

Cox hires new employees nearly every week of the year. Now she no longer worries about how to pay the rent and still buy food, of course, but she has lost none of the zest of that enthusiastic young woman who hoofed around Wilmington leaving a trail of business brochures.

"I feel there is no limit to our growth," Cox concludes. "I have met all the goals I set so I have to set new ones, like expanding our corporate offerings and finding a larger headquarters. I am just doing what I believe in and love, and I am working hard at it. To me, it is really that simple a formula and my biggest secret to success."

# Chapter 6

## Pioneering Educational Software

### Davidson and Associates, Inc.

*Publishing exciting educational software for children*

**Dr. Jan Davidson, Founder**

When Jan Davidson launched Davidson and Associates, Inc. in Torrance, California, in 1982, few people had heard of educational software. The market for such products was in its infancy, and only a few stores even sold computers. Home computers were considered the toys of hobbyists. In fact, some people feared that computer use would make children less human, more robotic.

All Davidson, a college English teacher, had going for her was an idea, the passion and energy to pursue it, and a few thousand dollars in savings. With these assets plus good business instincts and the able assistance of her husband, Bob, she built a dynamic company with annual revenues exceeding $200 million. In the process, she helped shape an industry that has revolutionized the learning process.

There were advantages to being an early entrepreneur in an emerging industry. According to Davidson, "We didn't have the baggage of a fixed business model and practices. We had the opportunity to make mistakes before anyone else did and learn from those mistakes, to try lots of "stuff" and keep what worked."

As it turned out, plenty of the "stuff" worked. Davidson and Associates' initial three products — Math Blaster, Word Attack, and Speed Reader — were featured on the first software best-seller list in 1983 and remain strong sellers today. By 1996, when the Davidsons sold their company for more than $1 billion, Davidson and Associates, Inc. was an award-winning leader in the fields of educational and entertainment software, with hundreds of successful products to its credit.

## Harnessing Excitement for Learning

Davidson's interest in education surfaced early in childhood. At age twelve, she began tutoring neighborhood youngsters for seventy-five cents an hour in the basement of her family's Indiana home. "It was then that I experienced my first 'aha' moment, that magical moment of understanding when a student's eyes brighten and the face displays that special expression, 'I get it.' I was hooked. Getting the 'ahas' became addictive. And it was always fascinating to me how some people could get things one way and others 'got it' another way," she says.

Davidson went on to earn bachelor's and master's degrees in communication from Purdue University and a doctorate in American Literature at the University of Maryland. While Bob rose through the ranks as an executive of an engineering company, Jan spent fifteen years teaching.

The idea of using computers as a learning tool dawned on her in the late 1970s as she watched her children and their friends play computer games on an early Apple computer. "I was struck by how excited and engaged they were by the interactive process," she says. "These computer games completely captured the kids' attention — a task that as a teacher I knew was no small feat." This was a new "aha" experience, and once more Davidson was hooked.

At the time, she was director of Upward Bound, a nonprofit learning center she founded in Palos Verdes, California. She searched high and low for software that would combine the thrill of computer games with the educational content her students needed to prepare themselves for the Scholastic Aptitude Test. When she found nothing suitable, she designed some simple games of her own with the help of a programmer.

Davidson tested her creations on her students, tweaking and revising the games to maximize fun and learning. "Before we knew it, parents, teachers, and students wanted to purchase them," she recalls.

The next step was to find a software publisher. As it turned out, good fortune disguised as bad luck intervened. One Saturday in September 1982, Davidson and her husband arrived at Tiny Naylor's, a San Clemente, California, restaurant. They were scheduled to meet with the head of a San Diego publishing firm and iron out details of a deal. Unbeknownst to them, however, the publisher had gone to a different Tiny Naylor's restaurant on the other side of town.

While they waited, Bob challenged his wife's plans to turn her software over to someone else to publish and market. "How can you do this? It's like giving your children up for adoption. No one understands your mission like you do," he argued, reminding her that software publishers of the day lacked her background in education, knowledge of presentation, and conviction in the promise of computers in learning.

"I can be a teacher or a software publisher — but not both," Jan maintained.

"But what is it you want to do?" Bob asked. When Jan replied that she wanted to be a teacher, he persisted, "Is that your goal, or is that your strategy? What is it you really want to do?"

"Help people learn," she replied.

"Well, won't you help people learn with educational software?" he urged. That day the couple left the restaurant united in purpose and never rescheduled the meeting with the publisher.

Years later, Jan spiced up many speeches by recounting this anecdote and thanking her husband for winning the argument. Once Bob had helped her see the crucial distinction between a goal and a strategy, she no longer felt guilty about "abandoning" teaching to publish educational software.

### Product Testing through Play

The Davidsons' start-up capital was $6,000 in savings that they had earmarked for their children's college educations. Jan wasted no time putting the money to good use. On her birthday, February 23, 1983, the first Math Blaster software went on the market. In less than six months, she had arranged for the manufacture, documentation, packaging, marketing, and distribution of her popular learning game. With each new product, she got better and faster at accomplishing these essential tasks.

The company's first-year revenues were approximately $200,000. "Profits are the lifeblood of any company," notes Davidson. "Every quarter, from day one, Davidson and Associates, Inc. has been profitable. We consistently achieved a 30 percent margin. One of our secrets, which few people have learned very well in the technology business, is to be diligent about carefully managing the expense side of the business. You can only project revenues, but you can control costs."

The company matured rapidly, in part due to Davidson's propensity for hiring smart, talented people whose professional objectives matched those of the company. "Goals are fixed; strategies are flexible," she points out, stressing that her role as president was to make the goals crystal clear. "We didn't rely only on salaries, bonuses, stock options, and other benefits to get the best people. We attracted them with opportunities to learn, develop, and grow, and a supportive environment that would allow them to be successful contributors not only to our purpose of helping people learn but to profits as well. Then we let the teams explore, evolve, and pursue the strategies. This required risk-taking, commitment, and fun."

Part of the fun involved the testing of new computer software products. Ordinary school children, the company's ultimate consumers, were invited to play with each new learning game on computers set around a brightly decorated glassed-in observation room. "We videotaped their faces, and we could tell by their reaction if they were enjoying something," says Davidson. This provided crucial business data while supplying her with a perpetual source of fresh "aha" moments.

Meanwhile Davidson was working hard to create a market for and improve distribution of educational software. She joined the Software Publishers' Association, serving on the board for ten years and as president part of the time. "We worked collaboratively to broaden our base of customers. For example, we founded Computer Learning Month to increase public awareness of the benefits of computers and learning," she explains.

## Surviving Industry Consolidation

By 1989, Davidson and Associates' revenues approached $10 million. "It became clear that there was an industry, and we were part of it. Our new purpose evolved into defining the right business model," Davidson says. With more opportunities in the offing than she could handle as president, she recruited her husband as the company's chairman and CEO.

Bob, an experienced and farsighted executive, predicted that the still immature software industry would consolidate from more than a hundred publishers to a handful of major companies. As a result of these predictions, the Davidsons set their sights on ensuring that Davidson and Associates, Inc. would survive as a major player. The new challenge was to develop the company into a leading multimedia studio with multiple sources of quality products and a strong distribution system.

To achieve this goal, the Davidsons began to strengthen their marketing relationships with consumer software outlets and schools. Further, they accelerated their development of home-grown products. They also acquired other development centers and entered into partnerships to form new product lines. For example, they began manufacturing and distributing educational software produced by other companies, such as Simon & Schuster, and coproducing with Fisher-Price interactive CD-ROMs for preschoolers .

In addition, the Davidsons took the adventurous step of entering into the entertainment side of the business by acquiring Blizzard Software, producers of the popular Warcraft 1, Warcraft 2, and Diablo games. In 1993, after careful soul-searching, they went public with the company. Soon Davidson and Associates, Inc. had 700 employees working to create, oversee the development of, and market up to thirty-three new titles every year.

About this time, the company's success made it an attractive target for larger corporations interested in the flourishing software industry. Thus far, the Davidsons had managed to stay a step ahead of the industry consolidation that Bob had predicted in 1989, but they knew they could not out race it forever. In autumn 1995, CUC International (now Cendant Corporation), a Connecticut-based telephone and Internet marketing company, began courting Davidson and Associates, Inc. and in July 1996, the Davidsons agreed to a stock swap that enabled CUC to acquire their company, in addition to Sierra OnLine, Inc., another software company. The Davidsons' share of the deal was valued at $1.15 billion.

"A lot of companies are ending up in places they didn't necessarily want to be," Bob said at the time. "This merger puts us in a position to control our own destiny."

Unfortunately, the Davidsons' destiny didn't run parallel to that of CUC International for long. A few months after the acquisition, "differences of opinion" with the new owners regarding goals and values prompted the couple to resign from the board and leave the company. They remained busy, however, having established The Davidson Foundation and The Davidson Group to handle substantial philanthropic and investment activities involving education and technology.

## A New Focus on Philanthropy

Jan's work continued to be her main hobby. "I'm dividing my time between philanthropy and helping to develop new education-related businesses," she explains. "Our role is advising. It's pretty exciting."

One of these companies, called Neurosmith, is combining advanced computer chip technology with the latest research in neuroscience to create a set of forty-one "smart toys" for kids from birth to age five. Another, called Brilliant Beginnings, is developing products for parents and day care providers that focus on the cognitive development of very young children.

Among her philanthropic efforts, Davidson serves as director of the Los Angeles County Educational Foundation, as a regent of the Board of Pepperdine University, as a fellow of the Claremont Graduate University, on the FCC and the DOE task force to implement the integration of technology and telecommunications in the nation's schools and libraries, and on the advisory board for the president's "America Reads Challenge."

The philanthropic activity that Jan feels most passionate about is nurturing and serving the special needs of profoundly gifted young people. In 1999, she and Bob formed the Davidson Institute for Talent Development (www.davidson-institute.org) to provide individualized educational and developmental programs for these children. "Although gifted children are one of society's greatest assets, little is being done to support these young learners," Jan notes. "And the research is clear that exceptional learners both below and above the mean require individualized, special provisions to meet their unique educational needs." In addition to the Davidson Young Scholars Program and Davidson Fellows Awards, the Institute will be launching a Virtual Learning Community for profoundly gifted young people. "Technology is a perfect way to allow these children to learn at their own pace, in their own style, and an opportunity to connect with each other as well," she says. Thus, in philanthropy as well as business, Davidson continues to use technology to facilitate learning.

Davidson is nationally recognized for her contributions to education. In addition to numerous other awards, she has been recognized as Woman Entrepreneur of the Year, awarded the American Academy of Achievement's Golden Plate of Excellence and the EDNET Hero Award for Significant Impact on Education through Technology, and has been inducted into the Technology Hall of Fame. Moreover, she has received an Honorary Doctorate of Law from Pepperdine University and an Honorary Doctorate of Education from Purdue University.

Davidson has distilled her experiences into some crisp and cogent advice for the educator with a marketable idea and an entrepreneurial bent. Ever the teacher, she sprinkles her comments with quotes, such as a favorite by F. Scott Fitzgerald: "The test of a first-rate intelligence is the ability to hold two opposed ideas in the mind at the same time, and still retain the ability to function."

"This applies to business," Davidson notes. Examples of seemingly opposed ideas that she has come to consider essential include: having a fixed goal while pursuing flexible strategies, establishing a clear sense of direction while encouraging experimentation and risk-taking, setting well-defined areas of responsibility while allowing operational autonomy, investing in the long term while demanding short-term performance, and focusing on purpose as well as profits.

Davidson continues to think ahead of the curve. "Teachers have been drilled into believing there is no other strategy," she says, noting that they must learn to think differently if they are to pursue their passion in a world bursting with opportunities.

"We can anticipate that learners who get their morning news on the Internet, customized to their interests and needs, in a format that best serves them are likely to expect a curriculum customized to their learning needs and objectives," Davidson explains. "Are they going to understand why they have no choice and must learn according to a standardized, one-size-fits-all curriculum? As our students needs and expectations change, we must change our educational practices to accommodate them."

# Chapter 7

## Making Learning Fun

### TREND enterprises, Inc.

*Promoting exciting learning environments*

**Kay Fredericks, Founder**

The office of Kay Fredericks — founder, chairperson, and CEO of TREND enterprises, Inc. in New Brighton, Minnesota — is tastefully decorated and visible from the corridor that serves as the main passageway for employees to get to their work stations. Through large unobstructed windows, Fredericks can be observed in her office by anyone in the corridor. This open atmosphere is typical of Fredericks's management style and sets the standard for openness within the organization.

Fredericks is a petite, soft-spoken, gracious, and articulate individual, who takes great pride in TREND's employees and customers. She radiates enthusiasm and a sense of dedication when discussing her company and its significance in helping educate children throughout the world.

"TREND's mission is to educate the children of the world by making learning fun," emphasizes Fredericks. "It is this vision that really inspires everybody throughout the company in every aspect of the work we do to make a difference in education." TREND employees believe that classroom surroundings and learning materials can make a difference, not only in how students feel but also in how they learn.

For over thirty years, TREND products have been used by teachers to create stimulating and enjoyable classroom environments, motivate and inspire young learners, and help teach basic skills. While the apparent strength of TREND's product line is its visual appeal, TREND's sound educational content and consistent high quality have earned the company many awards and loyal customers. The company offers products in four categories: Room Environments, Skill Builders, Awards and Incentives, and Teachers' Essentials.

The Room Environments category features products designed to enhance a classroom or learning environment with bright colors, dynamic images, and messages that motivate and teach. These products include bulletin board sets and timelines related to curriculum areas and holidays; unique posters; charts; and big, bright banners. Precut Ready Letters®, Terrific Trimmers®, Bolder Borders®, and Cultural Trimmers® add fun and colorful touches to these teaching displays.

TREND's Skill Builders make it fun and easy for children from three to thirteen to build confidence as they learn and practice important language arts and math skills. Products include flash cards; award-winning skill games including the popular learning Bingo format, which Fredericks originated in 1969; and reusable Wipe-Off® Activity Books, Cards, and Mats. Fredericks is especially proud to show off TREND'S five new lines of books for classroom and home use. These include teacher resource books filled with activities to inspire creative thinking and learning, plus an engaging series of Wickleville Woods Storybooks, where colorful cartoon animals star in character-building adventures.

TREND's Awards and Incentives category is built on the belief that children do better if they are motivated and recognized for their efforts, according to Fredericks. Teachers and parents can choose certificates, awards, and diplomas to celebrate everyday victories and major accomplishments. Perhaps TREND's most popular products are its hundreds of sticker titles, from dazzling Sparkle Stickers® to popular Scratch 'n Sniff Stinky Stickers®. Children especially enjoy these interactive, fragrant stickers because they are colorful and have scents ranging from popcorn to peppermint. "People of all ages love stickers!" says Fredericks. "One customer recently told us, 'I received your stickers as a child in school, and now I'm giving them to my students.' It's wonderful to know TREND is making learning fun for new generations of children."

TREND's Teachers' Essentials category features basic items that are made special with the unique TREND art style and value-added features, such as reusable Wipe-Off® surfaces. Wipe-Off Charts, Maps, and Calendars, name tags, incentive charts, and storage products are a few of the items you will find in classrooms all across the country.

An international company with over a thousand products is not what Fredericks imagined when TREND began more than thirty years ago. The idea for TREND grew out of her background as a creative kindergarten teacher. She graduated with a BS degree in education from St. Cloud State University in Minnesota. Although she did some graduate work, she did not pursue a graduate degree. Her only preparation for business came later as on-the-job training, attending workshops and seminars, and devouring business publications.

As a kindergarten teacher, the classroom environment was very important to Fredericks. To inspire her students, she created colorful cutout figures and characters about two and a half feet high to cover the wall-to-wall bulletin boards in her classroom. At the time, there was little if anything commercially available to create the attractive learning environment she felt was necessary for her students. The children loved the figures that were the same size as they were. Fredericks's cutout figures soon became the envy of her fellow teachers. Teachers from all over the school district would visit her classroom and ask, "Where did you buy the bulletin board cutouts?" After she explained that she had made them herself, they would request that she make bulletin board displays for their classrooms too.

### Designing Livelier Classrooms

Once Fredericks had been asked to make displays for other teachers, she began considering how she could produce them commercially. Making bulletin board materials for teachers was planted in her mind. In 1968, while recuperating from injuries resulting from a car accident, she had the opportunity to think more seriously about how she could help teachers who wanted to liven up classroom environments. She decided to begin making the life-size cutouts for her colleagues.

Fredericks recovered from her injuries, returned to teaching, and started the part-time business together with her former husband and their entire $700 savings account. In a relative's basement, she used a homemade silk-screen press to run off copies of the images. Simple brochures were mailed to teacher lists obtained from state departments of education throughout the United States. Mailing labels were created by Fredericks, using a typewriter her parents had given her in seventh grade. Initially, the product offering was less than a dozen bulletin board sets. Would teachers be interested in this new product? The answer came a week later, when Fredericks checked her post office box… and took home two large post office bags filled with orders from teachers all over the country. TREND enterprises, Inc. was born!

## Creating Reusable Products

After seven years of teaching and growing the business part-time, Fredericks took a leave of absence for two years to decide whether she wanted to leave the classroom and dedicate herself to TREND. In 1974, she resigned her teaching position and committed herself full-time to the business. At first, banks turned down Fredericks's loan requests because she did not have a formal business plan or the necessary collateral. Undaunted, she presented her product line and current customer list, finally convincing a bank that TREND could indeed succeed. She was rewarded with a credit line that helped launch TREND as a national company.

The name TREND was selected by Fredericks and a graphic designer while sitting around a kitchen table discussing the company. When the graphic designer asked what the company wanted to accomplish, it was stated that the company sought to create a trend in education and be a trendsetter for teachers, thus the business's name.

In the beginning, TREND was not taken very seriously, because Fredericks was young, a kindergarten teacher without any business background, and a woman in a male-dominated industry. In the 1960s and early 1970s, women entrepreneurs were rare, especially educational entrepreneurs, and veterans in the industry viewed Fredericks as inexperienced and lacking the necessary knowledge to succeed... not to mention the fact that her products were untried in the educational market. However, her tenacity and determination, together with a growing and impressive product line, soon began to make an impact on the industry.

Initially, the marketing was done through direct mail, with brochures and catalogs sent to teachers and schools nationwide. Dealer networks were also established through the National School Supply and Equipment Association, a national trade organization of retailers and manufacturers. Later, advertising pages were placed in large dealer catalogs as well as teacher magazines. TREND products were also displayed at educational conferences. Soon the company was receiving orders from all over the United States, and rapid growth was underway.

One reason for the company's success was the careful attention paid to product concept and design. A major strategy of TREND enterprises was to create products that teachers could reuse for their bulletin boards. This was the result of Fredericks's frustrating experience in discovering that products she purchased as a teacher often were not reusable. Moreover, TREND's products were designed to be attractive to children, durable, and practical for frequent use in the classroom. TREND was the first company in the industry to design brightly colored packaging for instructional products and the first to create products that have become industry standards: bulletin board sets, precut Ready Letters®, and Terrific Trimmers®.

## Products for Positive Reinforcement

Fredericks states that two critical decisions led to her success as an entrepreneur. The first was to leave teaching and focus full-time on the business, specifically product development. The other decision was to expand the product lines so that TREND could capture dominant market share in certain segments, such as room environment materials, skill-building games for children, and items that provided positive reinforcement for students.

After Fredericks realized that teachers were asking for materials that provided positive feedback for their students, TREND created its unique new category of stickers that focused on positive, motivational messages. Teachers could use these stickers to encourage good behavior and reward excellent work. In the 1980s, a pivotal decision in the company's growth came from 3M technology. The 3M Company, also headquartered in Minnesota, invited TREND to create a product that utilized their fragrance microencapsulation technology. This resulted in TREND's popular Stinky Stickers® line. These stickers when scratched, emit a tantalizing aroma. . . a runaway favorite with children. Two years after their introduction, over one million TREND Stinky Stickers® were sold!

As with any business, TREND has been through reorganization as well as fluctuations in sales. In the mid-1980s, Fredericks bought out her former husband and business partner to become sole owner of TREND enterprises, Inc. She emphasizes, "I learned that a fifty-fifty partnership is difficult because no one has a majority stake and neither person can have the final say. When there is a partnership, it is essential that the partners share common goals, values, and vision, and have a formal mechanism for settling differences in a nondestructive way."

Also in the mid 1980s, TREND lost market share after competitors obtained confidential information vital to the company's competitive advantage. Sales dropped 45 percent, and twelve employees had to be laid off. Fredericks and the TREND team got through this difficult time by working long hours, making good decisions, taking appropriate actions, and never losing confidence. Then TREND once again became a viable company and assumed its leadership role in the education market.

Fredericks has been forced to confront many other challenges as well. As the company continues to prosper, there is increased need to understand what the growth means and how it impacts systems, procedures, legalities, financing, and human resources, including compensation and benefits. Fredericks says, "There are always glitches and challenges along the way. I have been grateful for the many blessings that have allowed us to recover from stumbles and mistakes, regroup, and move forward again. I believe much of our success throughout the years comes from the quality of our people and their belief in our mission, as well as their passion to work things out regardless of difficulties and challenges."

Although Fredericks admits she sometimes misses teaching, especially relating with students and school colleagues, she loves what she is doing at TREND. She believes that many qualities good teachers possess are also very useful in the business world, namely organizational skills, patience, the ability to analyze problems, and the ability to bring out the best in others.

Fredericks says one of her greatest rewards in business is seeing TREND products make a difference in children's lives. She enjoys receiving accolades from teachers about how the products have transformed their classrooms, motivated children, and enriched the learning experience. Moreover, she believes being an entrepreneur has also enhanced her personal life. According to Fredericks, "I see things very differently, in a much wider scope than I would have if I had not had the entrepreneurial experience. I certainly appreciate all the work that goes into a given product in a way that I would never have otherwise known. My family chuckles whenever I receive a gift, because I spend as much time on the box and the packaging as I do on the gift itself."

She is especially proud that TREND is an equal opportunity employer, employing differently-abled people to assist with product packaging. Her company also reflects her dedication to helping women in business. TREND has many women department managers, and several women work on the manufacturing floor performing nontraditional roles, such as running forklifts and automated collators.

Over the years, Fredericks has been recognized by numerous organizations for her contributions to the education of children, for excellence in business, and for her community work. TREND enterprises, Inc. has been rated number one for sales volume, service, and manufacturing by *Educational Dealer Magazine.* Fredericks received the 1997 Lifetime Achievement Award and 1991 Business Owner of the Year Award from the National Association of Women Business Owners. She was honored by St. Cloud State University in 1991 with the Distinguished Alumni Award. In 1998, she received the Educational Dealers Supply Association's International Golden Apple Award for her "many contributions to education."

In addition to her many awards, Fredericks has served her community and the nation in various capacities. She was the first woman in the United States to lead a major metropolitan council for the Boy Scouts of America when she served as president of the Indianhead Council headquartered in St. Paul, Minnesota. Further, for eight years she has served as a member of the board of trustees for Hamline University, Minnesota's oldest and largest teacher training college, and was chairperson of the board for four years. She was a member of Advantage Minnesota, a group of legislators and government agency people, entrepreneurs, and corporate individuals who met regularly with the goal of developing and expanding the entrepreneurial base in Minnesota. She is also on the board of directors for a community bank and on the board of Norris Educational Innovations, Inc. (NEII). Fredericks values her community service as being very beneficial to her life and, in many ways, serving as her "PhD program." She feels that being on committees and boards has given her an opportunity to learn from experienced leaders who have been successful in their own professional spheres.

Today TREND employs more than 200 people. There is a sense of family among the employees of TREND. Fredericks states, with pride, "We talk a lot about being family and work hard at trying to know one another, not only by name but also by knowing something about each other. We keep connected. As TREND has grown, it has taken more effort to perpetuate a family atmosphere. Since we now have twenty different languages spoken among our employees, keeping connected is more important than ever before."

Staying connected also means sharing TREND's success with others. TREND makes many charitable contributions in a variety of ways, from product donations to employee volunteer efforts. "We look for opportunities to benefit children from ages three to thirteen," says Fredericks. "It's another way for us to have a positive impact on children's lives." One such opportunity came in 1997, when TREND decided to help area children by organizing a massive product donation to the flood victims in the Red River Valley of northern Minnesota and North Dakota. TREND employees came up with the idea and worked with Red River Valley school district officials to organize a plan. As a result, over $300,000 in TREND educational products were distributed to teachers whose classrooms were damaged or destroyed by the flood.

The company's products, numbering more than 1,000, are sold in forty-three countries, including the United States, Canada, Mexico, Great Britain, Japan, Korea, Greece, Australia, New Zealand, and South Africa. According to Fredericks, TREND's reputation as an outstanding educational company is a direct result of its products making a real difference in educating children. Fredericks sums it up this way: "If you look at our entire product line, you will see basic themes that run through all of our products — among them, multiethnicity, multiculturalism, promotion of self-esteem, environmental awareness, and gender balance. Our materials are bright, colorful, visual, easy to use, and fun. We believe these ideas and products transcend national boundaries. Our goal is to reach children everywhere, and reach them early in their lives, to show them that learning can be fun. . . and that they can succeed in school and in life."

# Chapter 8

## Realizing Educational Flexibility

### Innovative Education Management

*Establishing a network for homeschooling*

**Randy P. Gaschler, Founder**

Entrepreneurship is never for the faint of heart. But when one chooses to blaze a new trail, the challenges can be especially daunting. So it was for Randy Gaschler, whose first three years at the helm of Horizon Instructional Systems, a northern California charter school for students who learn primarily through a combination of homeschooling, independent study, and small classes, could be characterized as the best of times and the worst of times.

Gaschler's varied background prepared him for most of the challenges he would confront. The rest he managed to surmount through hard work, on-the-job learning, and the support of parents and key officials.

After playing football and earning a degree in economics from the University of California at Los Angeles (UCLA), Gaschler served briefly as a college football coach, built homes for a while, was a cabinetmaker for four years, and owned and operated an auto parts store for seven years before going to night school in 1989 to get the teaching credentials he had always wanted.

In 1990, he was hired to coach football and teach social studies at a high school in Lincoln, California. Then when the Western Placer School District was forced to lay off teachers in 1991 due to declining enrollment, Gaschler lost his social studies slot. But out of adversity came opportunity and inspiration. To keep Gaschler on as coach, the district put him in charge of overseeing its homeschooling and independent study program. However, he quickly became dissatisfied with the public school system's method of funding and providing education for students who didn't fit its traditional program. Gaschler empathized with these students' needs and their parents' dilemmas. Gaschler's wife had homeschooled two of their children when finances were tight, and the couple had had to fight to get one of their sons into a public school classroom where the teacher's approach was sufficiently structured for the boy. Eventually, all five of their children ended up in private schools that offered greater programmatic flexibility.

To further educate himself about alternatives in education, Gaschler, who considers himself a lifelong learner, spent considerable time reading the local library's books on the subject. The information he acquired supported his own personal experience and was a catalyst for his next career move.

"I was stunned that there was so much difference of opinion out there about how children learn best. Everybody's approach worked for somebody, but it was obvious to me that nobody knew the best way. My next thought was that no one should be deciding which philosophy is tried on which kid except the parent, because if an approach doesn't work, the parent bears the brunt of it," Gaschler says.

## Exploring the Charter School Option

In March 1993, a local school principal met with Gaschler to discuss California's newly implemented law permitting the establishment of charter schools and suggested he explore the option for the district. Gaschler welcomed the possibility of introducing more flexibility into public education, and drafted a charter that would give parents the freedom to choose the curriculum and learning strategies that best suited their children.

The charter identified general goals for students in seven growth areas: literacy, life skills, history, political science, mathematics, science, and special interests. Progress was to be measured not by time spent on a subject, but according to mastery. Students would have their work monitored and evaluated by a certified teacher called an education specialist. A parent could request a different teacher at any time, and a teacher could ask to be relieved from supervising any given student.

"I talked to some parents about it, and they thought it was a good plan," Gaschler says. "Then I presented it to the district superintendent, and he was concerned about financial issues. We negotiated a contract that would protect the district from losing money if this thing was wildly successful and all the kids wanted to go to our school. I wanted to be able to enroll kids from other districts, and I wanted Western Placer School District to front us the money we would be entitled to, based on enrollments, so we could meet initial payroll and other expenses."

Once such business arrangements had been made, the charter went to the Board of Education, which approved it in June 1993. That fall, Horizon Instructional Systems opened with twenty-five students from the district's existing home study program, all enrolled through responses to inquiries rather than through advertising. By the end of the first year, Horizon Instructional Systems had enrolled over 600 students.

Because Gaschler had no degree in school administration, he had to teach himself the intricacies of educational funding. Under state law, the charter schools receive funds for each enrolled student, based on an Average Daily Attendance (ADA) formula. In theory, because such schools are not required to provide brick-and-mortar facilities, they can do more educating with the money. Horizon Instructional Systems chose to use a substantial portion of the ADA money ($1000 at first) for each student to be used by the teacher to develop an individualized learning plan.

These instructional funds are spent by mutual agreement between the parents and the teachers to customize education for students. They have been used to finance things like books, educational equipment and supplies, computers and software, a student's share of small group classes (such as algebra, science, English, piano, karate, Spanish), and other educational activities or products.

Another large portion of Horizon Instruction Services' ADA allocation is used to pay teachers, who receive an annual salary based on the number of students they supervise, the kinds of duties they perform, and the length of time they have worked at the school. Other ADA monies go to administer the program, including nonteacher salaries, bookkeeping and auditing, the development and maintenance of an Internet-based communication system, the updating of a list of approved vendors of educational supplies and equipment, the monitoring of education-related laws and policies, and the administering of a state-mandated test.

In the beginning Gaschler worked grueling hours to get Horizon Instructional Systems up and running. It was headquartered in an office that was part of a small trailer, and since he had no secretary at first he hired teachers, answered questions from parents, taught himself how to set up and maintain computer databases, and hooked up two modems to establish a bulletin board system for communicating with the many schools serviced by the company.

However, what might have looked chaotic to someone accustomed to the routines and procedures of traditional schools seemed appropriately evolutionary to Gaschler. In fact, his vision prevented him from letting administrative convenience and uniformity place constraints on educational flexibility. "In the beginning, we had no manuals, no policy," he recalls. "I wanted to create a process based on what was good education. Each problem and issue was thought through. We developed a rationale or answer based on parental choice, individualizing instruction for each kid."

## Emphasizing Individualized Instruction

During the first year, Horizon Instructional Systems attracted 660 students. The operation was so successful — and the entire concept of charter schools was so new and controversial — that the school also attracted the attention of the California Department of Education. Unfortunately for Gaschler, who admits to having been a political neophyte, most of that attention resulted in negative reactions. "A couple of people from the Department of Education came in and told us that we were out of compliance," recounts Gaschler. "They said we couldn't spend a thousand dollars on each student for supplies because our school district was only spending eighty dollars per student. They said we couldn't check out computers to our students in their homes because the district didn't do that. They said we couldn't pay for classes that had as few as five or six students because that student-to-teacher ratio was lower than the one in regular classrooms. And we said, 'What are you talking about? This is the intent of the law; this is something new.'"

By October of the second year, Horizon Instructional Systems was even more successful yet also more controversial. Enrollment had grown to 1,300, but after more battling with the Department of Education, the district's board of trustees said it would revoke the school's charter in mid-March 1995.

This was an extremely painful period for Gaschler, personally as well as professionally. While newspapers and the district superintendent were labeling him a thief of public funds, his wife left him and his church closed. But he refused to give up, even though there was a real risk the school would be shut down.

Fortunately, a last-ditch rally in the capital by about 500 parents and students, plus the support of a key state senator, led to a temporary reprieve. Major matters like Horizon Instructional Systems' ability to receive and spend funds, however, remained in limbo. The school was still in operation, but continued to be controversial and threatened.

Soon the tide began to turn in the school's favor. First, the author of the original charter school legislation wrote a letter saying that the Department of Education's interpretation was wrong. Then, the state attorney general issued an opinion to that effect. Finally, the Western Placer School District lent its support by threatening to file suit against the state.

In March 1996, a settlement was reached that allowed Horizon Instructional Services to remain open. In Gaschler's opinion, the agreement also clarified issues about the charter school movement in California. "It said that if it were legal for a regular school to do something, even if they weren't doing it because of financial constraints, then we could do it. And that is all we wanted," he says.

Horizon has continued to grow. In 1999, it had 3,200 students in six northern California counties served by 150 teachers. Meanwhile, Gaschler's administrative system, while still geared toward permitting maximum flexibility, has become quite sophisticated. For example, he has developed a database program to track the status of every purchase order and document the current location of every item bought. The system can also determine whether a consumable item has been used up, to whom each computer and piece of equipment has been issued, and whether a used textbook has been returned to a teacher's inventory or was purchased at a discount by another student's instructional fund.

Gaschler had committed early on to make full use of online technology. This not only has facilitated distance learning by students but has enabled effective remote administration of the program. As a result, Gaschler was well positioned to take advantage of the 1998 amendment to the charter school statute that permits these schools to be managed by nonprofit corporations.

"In spring 1998, I went to Horizon's governance committee and said I believed the long-term success of our school would depend on having a number of schools like ours. If we grew to be one school of 50,000 kids, we would be taking a lot of political shots. But if there were fifty schools, all with 1,000 kids each and all being managed under the same principles, I thought we could gain the political clout that would be needed to fight the battles down the road," explains Gaschler.

Subsequently, with the support of the governance committee and concurrence of the school district, Gaschler established a nonprofit management company called Innovative Education Management (IEM), of which he is president. Gaschler sees many opportunities for growth, program enhancements, and managerial improvements in the future. For example, parents continue to support the establishment of new small group classes and other educational opportunities for students. And Gaschler plans to negotiate volume discounts from suppliers and centralize functions like bookkeeping. "This will allow us to reduce costs so we can increase what we spend directly on students," he says.

Gaschler also points to another innovation he expects to flourish: a Horizon site that has begun offering instruction for seven hours a day, five days a week, to serve twenty-five students. The parents wanted to retain control over their children's education, but were unable or chose not to homeschool the children or provide close study supervision. Gaschler predicts that, under the management of IEM, additional all-day sites will emerge in the next five years.

"We will be a threat at that point, because people who can't have their kids at home will be able to send their kids to our sites. My goal is to threaten the traditional public schools so badly that they will do what we are doing — start managing their money better, individualizing their instruction, and incorporating what parents want done for their kids," he states. As these comments clearly reveal, Gaschler's commitment to flexibility, individualization, creativity, and parental involvement in education remains as strong as ever.

# Chapter 9

## Providing Access to Teaching Tools

### ERASER DUST and ALPHA TEACHING TOOLS

*Educational stores for students, teachers, and parents*

**Cynthia P. Huereque, Founder**

With only a vision of service, in 1985 Cynthia Huereque, assisted by her husband Eric and her family, established Eraser Dust, a very successful retail business selling school supplies and materials in El Paso, Texas. Today, that business has grown to four retail stores in Texas (three in El Paso and one in Houston) as well as a branch store, Alpha Teaching Tools, in Las Cruces, New Mexico. This New Mexico store was already in existence and was purchased by Huereque in 1990. Because the name Eraser Dust was unknown in New Mexico, it was decided to keep the original name. All of these stores offer a similar array of educational games, children's books, art supplies, computer learning programs, workbooks, bulletin board suggestions, office supplies, puzzles, stickers, certificates, gifts, and children's music and videos, CDs, posters, and motivational banners — pretty much anything a teacher, parent, or grandparent might want use to excite and enhance a child's learning. Today, Eraser Dust and Alpha Teaching Tools provide a virtual cornucopia of products that pique the imaginations of teachers as well as students.

One of the more fascinating facets about this business is that it is truly a family business. Eraser Dust and Alpha Teaching Tools currently employ thirty-four people, fourteen of whom are members of the extended Huereque family. Sons, daughters, sisters, brothers, daughters-in-law, nephews, and nieces are all active in the business. Cynthia's sister Irma and her husband are partners with Cynthia and her husband, Eric Huereque Sr. in the Houston store, while Cynthia's son, Eric Jr., manages the New Mexico store. Eric Jr. was able to take over the management of this store in 1990 when he was only nineteen, having been active in the business since age fourteen. In 1997, the family nature of the business was strengthened when Eric Jr. married Liza Ochotorena, who had been working at the store since 1993. Today, the couple is an effective management team in the Las Cruces store, where Eric focuses on merchandising and setting up displays while Liza focuses on customer service.

The majority of customers at all stores are teachers although an increasing number of parents and grandparents visit the stores each year. With an expanded customer base and changing customer needs, the Huereques continually reassess their products. Cynthia explains: "About seventy-five to eighty percent of our business comes directly from the public schools. We try to be ready for what they want and need. We have found that it is different in various states. For example, New Mexico wanted materials that would support thematic learning before it became popular in Texas. Now we have those materials in all our stores." While the emphasis is on offering supplies and materials consistent with the curriculum needs and standards of the of the area, all stores also carry a collection of materials appropriate for use in Sunday schools and vacation Bible schools. That decision not only was a business choice but also reflects the Christian values that permeate the Huereque family efforts.

## Materials for Individual Programs

Huereque's varied background in education was the catalyst for her to become an entrepreneur. She comes from a family with a deep respect for education and what it can do to improve people's lives. Huereque and her three sisters — all of whom are bilingual in Spanish and English — became teachers. After graduating from Austin High School in El Paso, Huereque attended the University of Texas at El Paso, where she earned a BA degree in education and a certification to teach English, science, health, and physical education. She taught for fifteen years, ten of which were spent teaching English, physical education, and science in a middle school in El Paso. She also taught special education for a small rural school while concurrently working toward a special education certificate. Following this, she taught for years at a local independent Christian school, Christian Heritage, where her three children were enrolled as students. As a teacher, Heuereque was constantly frustrated by the lack of easy access to the materials she felt she needed to do an excellent job. While the school furnished the essentials of books and supplies, and offered the means to order other teaching materials to provide individualized programs, obtaining them from catalogs was often difficult. Products were not always accurately described in the catalogs, and only one small local outlet offered any assistance while making a decision.

Consequently, in 1985 Huereque and one of her younger sisters opened the first Eraser Dust in El Paso — a small store of only 900 square feet on the city's west side. It was so successful that within six months they opened their second store in an outlet mall on the city's east side. At the end of that first year, Huereque's sister, deciding that retail was much more time-consuming than she had imagined, sold her half of the business to Huereque and her husband Eric, who with his family had run a successful dairy farm in the El Paso area.

Huereque sees her husband's business background as instrumental to the success of Eraser Dust. Cynthia reflects on how they established the business: "From the beginning it was a learning experience for both of us. Neither of us had any retail experience. I was a teacher, and Eric was a dairy farmer. He knew about business; I knew about education. We both knew that we wanted to work together. We both felt strongly about our city and wanted to continue to be a part of it. So we got a personal bank loan and began building the business. Fortunately, I did not have to take out what little retirement money I had put into the system."

## Business Success through Family Cooperation

In the fifteen years since the business was established, it has grown from one store to five. The three in El Paso vary in size from 900 square feet to the newest one on Lee Trevino Drive, named after the local golf hero, which has 7,600 square feet. Alpha Teaching Tools in Las Cruces, forty minutes from El Paso, is in a 5,500 square foot building. Houston Eraser Dust, the newest store, opened in 1996. The Houston store was first proposed by Huereque's sister as a business she wanted to operate after her retirement. Huereque recalls: "My sister Irma taught school in Houston for twenty-five years. She always asked me whether when she was ready to retire, she could open a store with me. I said, 'Sure, just let me know when, and we'll do it.' One day she called me and said she was ready. I told her to start looking for a place. Eric and I went over to Houston, talked with Irma and her husband, found a good location, formed a new partnership, and got started the year after Irma retired."

Although being in business with family members could be a disadvantage for some people, the Huereque family works harmoniously together, taking advantage of the strengths and weaknesses of the various family members. There is a definite division of labor within the company and within the family, but one that is rooted in trust. Eric Sr. serves as the business manager for the total operation, making sure there is a positive cash flow. Huereque herself does most of the purchasing for the company, although her sister Irma is the major buyer for the Houston store. The two sons who manage two of the El Paso stores are also active in purchasing for their stores. Huereque's brother is in charge of the warehouse. While people are primarily hired and fired by Huereque, the various managers participate in these processes. Concerning the family's unified efforts, Huereque remarks, "You might think that being so close to the family in the business would create problems. I guess it does sometimes, but those minor problems are quickly forgotten. I feel so fortunate that we can all work to do something that brings the family together. I really feel blessed. I think we all do."

The family members are aware of both the opportunities offered by their community and the obligations to the community in general and the schools in particular. Since their business is education oriented, each person in it pays close attention to what is going on in schools locally as well as nationally by attending conferences, workshops, and various sales presentations. They recognize that they must stay up-to-date, not only for their business but for the good of local educational programs as well. Moreover, they know that while most of their customers come from public schools, some have special needs, such as homeschoolers or participants in religious education programs.

Eraser Dust and Alpha Teaching Tools try hard to ensure good quality in all the products they carry. In addition to consulting with individual teachers, they also deal with individual schools and school districts by servicing purchase orders and responding to district bids. As Huereque explains: "We service a lot of purchase orders from all the districts. The standard orders for paper and school supplies go to larger wholesale suppliers. We often participate in some of the smaller requests for bids on specialty items. Remember, we are pretty much a mom-and-pop operation."

Besides actively participating in a variety of chambers of commerce, church groups, and professional organizations, members of the family are frequently called on to work in the schools. Huereque sums up their contributions to the community in these words: "We belong to several organizations — the El Paso Chamber of Commerce, the Hispanic Chamber of Commerce, the YMCA, and a variety of school partnership education programs. We go to science fairs or to classrooms just to read to the youngsters. We have often participated in school career days. I really like to keep in touch with what is going on. Visiting with students and teachers at the schools helps us get a much better idea of needs and interests. It also allows us to give something back to the community. We are active in our church, as well. My sister Irma and I are on the advisory board of the Steck Vaughn Company. All in all, we stay pretty busy."

## Breaking into Bilingual Education

In assessing needs for educational materials and deciding which ones Eraser Dust and Alpha Teaching Tools will focus on, Huereque feels especially strong about providing teachers and students with good materials. In detailing the need for such materials, she says, "We have a large bilingual population of teachers. Many teach in Spanish. We even get teachers from our border cities in Mexico. Several schools there teach in English, so these teachers come across to buy both bilingual materials and materials in English. Being able to better reach this special niche has been very rewarding, but there is a need for much more material. For example, we need something that adults can use for developing everyday communication skills."

Huereque constantly focuses on the future of her business and at the same time enthusiastically reflects on the past. She is proud of what she has already accomplished: "I guess knowing that I was able to get to this point in the business world is what is most satisfying to me. Starting with almost nothing and ending up with five stores makes me feel as though all the work has paid off. Recognizing that I did this as a woman and a minority one at that makes it even more special. Of course, doing it with the family is what matters most."

Like all educational entrepreneurs, Huereque knows that there have been rewards, but there also have been challenges and hardships running the family business. She reflects, "It wasn't easy, especially at first. As a teacher, I was used to living with a paycheck, primarily working from eight to four, having my weekends free, time off in the summer, and a health plan paid for. Then all of a sudden I had no paycheck and a twenty-four-hour-a-day job. I did have my own time and was boss, but that took a lot to get used to. I had to plan my days much differently. Sure the rewards are there, but it's not all a Cinderella story. Although I worked hard at school, I am working harder here, and I love it."

When asked what advice Huereque might give to future educational entrepreneurs, she was very clear. "Think about what you might do because you really have to love it. Be sure you have enough resources to last a few years with very little money coming back in. If you decide to go into retail, recognize that you will have to keep up with what is happening in education and be ready to provide good customer service. Remember that teachers, like everybody else, are price conscious. Be sure you can price your products fairly both to your customers and yourself. Also remember that your goal is to help kids learn. Teachers and parents will want your help. You may not be officially teaching, but you will have a chance to be an important part of the lives of many young people and their families."

These are good words of advice. They are worth thinking about whether one would choose retail or not. To follow Huereque's footsteps exactly, which is quite unlikely, one would certainly have to have a family that is ready, willing, and able to be there every inch of the way.

It is especially interesting to note that at the time of this writing, Huereque is opening a branch store in Juarez, Mexico. In year 2000, Eraser Dust became an international company — all in all a very satisfying step in entrepreneurship for Huereque and her family.

# Chapter 10

## Managing Innovative Schools

### Designs for Learning, Inc.

*Developing high-performance learning systems*

**Dr. Wayne B. Jennings, Founder**

Designs for Learning, a company committed to helping bring about positive changes in education, was established in 1987 when Dr. Wayne Jennings took an early retirement from the St. Paul, Minnesota, Public Schools. At the time he left the St. Paul District, Jennings was the director of staff development. During his career in the school district, he had served as a teacher and a principal of several "cutting edge" schools at various educational levels, including the St. Paul Open School, the Battle Creek Junior High School, and the Central High School. Throughout these years, Jennings challenged many traditions and explored numerous innovations.

Today, Designs for Learning, Inc. provides a wide variety of services for an equally wide range of clients. Under Jennings, the company manages four charter schools in the Twin Cities area. One, a K-5 school in St. Paul, educates over 130 students. Moreover, in cooperation with Concordia University, the company has developed and is managing another elementary school enrolling over 100 students. In 1998, the Inver Hill Community College and Designs for Learning, Inc. created the Minnesota

Technical High School, which has a strong focus on technology. And, with the Central Lakes Community College, Jennings and the company staff have created and manage a middle school designed for urban students that currently has an enrollment of two-thirds minority students. Together these schools employ over sixty teachers, teacher assistants, and onsite administrators. While all these schools are different in many ways, they also have similarities, such as a personal learning plan for each student, a small teacher-student ratio, a staffing pattern that includes paraprofessionals, an educational advisor for every fifteen students, and a twenty-five-day training program each year.

Designs for Learning, Inc. also has a variety of consultant and management contracts with school districts, agencies, and institutions of higher learning in several communities throughout the Midwest, the South, and California. Jennings and the president of Designs for Learning, Inc., Dr. J. David Alley, have consulted with the San Diego, California, Children's Museum to establish a very successful charter school for elementary grade students in that community. Moreover, Jennings and his ten full-time staff members have helped set up the High School for Recording Arts in St. Paul. They also assisted Options for Youth, a California organization, in setting up its first high school in Minnesota for at-risk students. These and other consultant contracts in education policy, in developing innovative learning systems, and in teacher, administrator, and board training continue to keep Designs for Learning, Inc. a vibrant company.

## Becoming a Change Agent

Every entrepreneurial program, product, or service reflects a personal vision. Designs for Learning, Inc. originated in Jennings's dreams. From the beginning of his teaching career in the St. Paul Public Schools, Jennings's search for ways to improve education led him to such responsibilities as designing the Saturn School of Tomorrow, the Children's Theatre School, The Mall of America High School, and the Expo Magnet Middle School, all successful St. Paul programs.

One of Jennings's most exciting projects was the establishment and direction of the St. Paul Open School, where he served as principal from 1971 to 1978. This K-12 research-based demonstration school has attracted over 20,000 visitors and has been described in over thirty articles and books. Moreover, the St. Paul Open School won the Pacesetter Award from the US Office of Education for being educationally effective, cost effective, and worthy of replication.

Throughout these years of varied experiences, Jennings established a consistent, research-based philosophy of teaching and learning that reflects his belief in and commitment to change. His convictions include respect for the individual, trust in people's ability to communicate, and recognition of the role of leadership in the change process. A few of his thirty-one directives for the change process are: "Recognize that change is more a commitment from people than new dollars," "Ask," "Ask again. Persist! Most change takes multiple efforts to persuade decision makers," "Look for partners," "Build trust," "Start. Don't spend too much time planning. You can think of all the reasons not to do it," "Provide for vision keepers," and "Live in the future."

Not surprisingly, a person with such awareness, understanding, and commitment to beliefs occasionally is at odds with more traditional leadership in education. When asked how he sees himself as an educator, Jennings replies, "Primarily, I see myself as a change agent. I think I have been a change agent throughout my career. Even when I was within the system, I was a change agent. But in the system I found that I had to play 'Captain May I,' and all too often the answer was 'no.' I found that I had to learn to be a schemer. Sometimes I had to be creatively disobedient and stay out of hot water so as not to get fired. Often I found my actions very limited."

## Contracting for Challenge

Jennings had spent almost thirty years with the St. Paul Schools when in 1987 he decided it was time to strike out on his own. Armed with his retirement money and the respect of many people in the district, he established Designs for Learning, Inc. Much of his initial work and income came from within the district. Soon the variety and quality of his teacher training programs and system and policy recommendations were recognized by neighboring school districts, and Designs for Learning, Inc. grew. New contracts resulted in new projects; new projects increased contacts; new contacts helped expand the range of offerings.

In growing his business, Jennings has not found it necessary to focus on extensive marketing, as he remarks: "Actually, we have done very little marketing. Originally I never did any. Work just came in. I was very active. People knew me. I knew lots of people. Word of mouth was very important. Most of our work came through our own initiative. We would go out and tackle a project, and the results would speak for themselves. Mailings helped a bit with marketing our charter school services at first, but for us the best exposure is word of mouth."

When Designs for Learning, Inc. was first established, everything was done out of Jennings's home. However, as the business grew, the office was moved to commercial property. According to Jennings, his big breakthrough came when Designs for Learning, Inc. became a winner of the New American Schools Project competition. He explains: "New American Schools was set up during President Bush's administration. It was established to try to work on school reform aside from the government doing it alone. A private nonprofit corporation was set up with the encouragement of the president. Honeywell, IBM, Boeing, and other large firms kicked in about $30 million to redesign American education. In a competition for teams to come up with a comprehensive design, over 700 applications were received from corporations, universities, and individuals across the country. Eleven proposals were selected, and ours was one of them. In fact, ours received the highest rating."

Winning that contract had a big impact on the development of Designs for Learning, Inc. Financially, it brought in $1 million each year for the next three years. However, while the money was important, having the resources to put together and test a concept that had previously been only a dream was even more important. As a result of the New American Schools funding, the concept was developed by the end of the first year, then for the following two years tested in the schools. The Community Learning Centers developed, put in place, and evaluated throughout this period of time held up well. Now Designs for Learning, Inc. had a time-tested model that translated perfectly to the charter school movement, which was beginning about the same time. Jennings remarks on this similarity: "It became immediately obvious that our Community Learning Center concept would easily and effectively form a basis for the development of a charter school. So, upon completion of that third year with the New American Schools project, we immediately set up our first such school. The success of that school not only led to the development of others for which we are totally responsible, it opened the doors for us to assist others as they got started."

Today, Jennings and Designs for Learning staff members in addition to administering their own charter schools, also work with other agencies to set up, manage, assess, and evaluate charter schools. In this way, the work established through the New American Schools program continues to impact America's education.

### Instilling Excitement about Change

In considering advice for future entrepreneurs establishing businesses, Jennings stresses the necessity of overcoming temporary difficulties and fear. Recalling his own experiences, he says, "It hasn't always been a bowl of cherries. There have been times when funding was a problem. Business was slow. We had to learn how to work differently, especially after the original high offered us by the New American Schools grant. We solved that with a line of credit from a local bank. We managed to keep ourselves alive and in increasingly good shape. That was certainly a time of worry and uncertainty."

While funding is often an issue for Jennings, finding good personnel is also a constant concern. It is interesting to Jennings that while the education profession attracts many fine committed people, they sometimes have a certain personality trait that makes it difficult for them to adjust to new educational ventures. He remarks, "There are an awful lot of people in education who are attracted by the safety and security the profession tends to offer. They somehow act as though everything is going to happen by magic. The check will be there because it flows from the public coffers. We have to help those people see that it won't always happen that way."

Another problem that Jennings identified was how to help people feel the need for change. Throughout his career, he has found that "pushing the envelope" or "thinking out of the box" is foreign to many educators. It is hard to help some people understand that there are alternative means of educating people.

Yet Jennings has discovered effective ways to help others desire transformation and alternatives in education. In his words, "We have developed an entire strategy for breaking down these barriers to change. We have developed a whole set of slogans and sayings we use to help present our perspective in a wide variety of writing and speaking opportunities. We have generated a series of public presentations that offer a thorough understanding of educational research consistent with new ideas in education. I have found that most people either don't know that research or have forgotten it. I have also found that having some personnel with PhDs has helped us with some problems. People seem to be more willing to listen if you have that degree. We use whatever mechanisms we can to reach people at an emotional or logical level, even a snob level if necessary." And those mechanisms have worked.

For Jennings and Designs for Learning, Inc., success has bred more success, reflected not only in the numbers of schools and programs offered, the number of staff employed, or the amount of money generated, but in the excitement Jennings feels every time he visits one of his schools. He reflects: "I get energy from the attitude of the teachers in our schools. They feel empowered. They say they are working the hardest they have ever worked, but they are enjoying it more. They are getting great feedback from parents about how well the children are doing. They feel they are part of a team — a team with clear objectives and sense of purpose. That is what keeps it exciting. I don't have to do this at all. I'm sixty-eight now. I've got a good pension. I could continue my teaching at St. Thomas and do more writing, speaking, and relaxing. But the rewards are too great. I'm seeing things happen that I have hoped for and dreamed about all my life as an educator. I'm not ready to give that up."

Throughout the years, Jennings has continued to focus on personal growth. He has served on literally dozens of boards and in a leadership capacity in several organizations. Furthermore, he publishes the Association of Supervision and Curriculum Development (ASCD) newsletter, *Brain Based Education/ Learning Styles Networker.* In 1988, he became an adjunct professor of education at the University of St. Thomas, a liberal arts school in St. Paul with which Jennings remains active. He has served as president of the Association of Educators in Private Practice and as president of the Minnesota Association of Charter Schools. He has also worked with such diverse groups as the Minnesota Futurists, the Minnesota Association of Alternative Programs, and the Minnesota Alliance for the Arts in Education. Currently, he holds board positions with the Center for Policy Studies, Public School Incentives, the Transforming Schools Consortium, Brain Based Education Network, and the Institute for Learning.

As for the future, Jennings is optimistic. He notes, "I have always been interested, aside from our little peanut-sized operation, in what we can do to change the world. There is great satisfaction for me in the possibility of change. It is extremely satisfying that many reform efforts have continued and accelerated. Now people are talking about choice, charter schools, and homeschooling. Opportunities for private entrepreneurs seem to be multiplying. Things are changing. Business groups and legislatures are pushing for change. I see this as a point of satisfaction. I am excited about what appears to be an endemic interest in educational change and reform. I'm glad I have lived long enough to not only see it but to be an active participant in it. I am a very lucky guy."

With his lifelong commitment to learning and his constant pursuit of ways to improve education in spite of risks, Jennings serves as a role model for future educational entrepreneurs. Jennings sums up the importance of personal growth and of making a difference in education in these words: "I find it continually amazing how people can stay in the profession and not grow. I don't understand what kind of joy or satisfaction they receive when they don't participate, share ideas, or reach out to help make something happen. I know it takes time. I know it takes energy. Some people say it takes sacrifice. I say even if this is true, it is more than worth it."

# Chapter 11

## Opting for Adventure in Education

### Shearwater Books, Ltd.

*Writing historical fiction, fairy tales, and fables*

**Dr. Eric A. Kimmel, Founder**

By all appearances, Eric A. Kimmel had it made in the early 1990s. The former elementary school teacher held a tenured professorship at Portland State University in Oregon, where he taught classes in what he calls "all the fun stuff," such as children's literature, language arts methods, and handwriting. But two developments pushed him toward a pivotal decision to radically change his career and exchange security for independence and creativity.

The first development was connected to finances. For more than two decades, Kimmel had pursued his dream of writing children's books on a part-time basis, specializing in historical fiction, fairy tales, and fables. For many of those years his income from this side venture was unpredictable and less than spectacular. But when he sat down to prepare his tax return in 1990, he was surprised to discover that his writing revenues nearly equaled his academic salary. As a result, he contacted an accountant, who advised him to incorporate.

The second development involved a nagging dissatisfaction with his day job. Although Kimmel enjoyed teaching, he loved storytelling. To his dismay, a new cooperative teaching model being implemented at Portland State required him to spend more hours than ever with colleagues and students — hours he was accustomed to devoting to his writing. "I was faced with the fact that I had two full-time jobs. I had to choose one or the other," he says. "'Security or adventure?' I asked myself. 'Which one do you want?' I chose adventure. I can't say I had a master plan. I dealt with issues as they occurred and solved them one at a time. I just decided not to teach anymore and be a writer. I went for it."

Kimmel has never regretted his decision. Of the nearly fifty children's books he has in print today, thirty were published after 1993, when he began to write full-time. In addition to researching and writing his books and magazine stories, the award-winning author and nationally recognized authority on children's literature spends fifty days or more each year on the road, speaking at schools, libraries, and conferences across the country. He captivates audiences by telling his stories and sharing inspirational and practical information about his craft.

Born in Brooklyn in 1946, Kimmel has vivid memories of sitting with his grandmother as she recounted stories, fairy tales, and fables of Eastern Europe. "I would listen for hours," he says. "I got an idea of what a good story is, how it works, how it's told, and how stories constantly change in the telling."

Books fascinated young Kimmel. He literally read his copy of *Grimm's Fairy Tales* to pieces. *Horton Hatches the Egg* by Dr. Seuss was another of his favorites. One day in kindergarten he was astounded when his teacher explained that books were written by people, and that any of the students might grow up to write a book, just like Dr. Seuss. "I thought, 'That's for me. Nothing could be as exciting as seeing my name on the cover of a book,'" recalls Kimmel. "It was as if I'd always known I'd be a writer."

Although tantalized by this dream, Kimmel did not make it a reality for some time. In high school he enrolled in one creative writing class that he enjoyed very much, and contributed to high school and college publications. But although a number of teachers praised his writing talents, no one urged him to make a living as a full-time author.

"Writing was looked down on when I was going to school,"

he explains. "It wasn't considered a career; it was on the level of being a juggler or something like that. In the 1960s, a career was being a doctor or lawyer."

Instead of focusing on writing initially, Kimmel opted to become an elementary school teacher. He received a BA degree from Lafayette College and taught in New York City for several years. Then he moved to the Virgin Islands and taught fifth grade briefly before taking a job as a librarian. Working in a library brought him into daily contact with the kinds of children's books he loved as a child.

One evening, while on night duty at the library, a patron returned a history book by a British author. "I still remember it; Phillip Longworth's *The Cossacks,*" Kimmel recalls. It looked interesting, so Kimmel picked it up and began reading it. As he turned the pages, he thought, "This information would make an interesting novel if I could come up with a good story." He remembers saying to himself, "I've always wanted to be an author. Dreaming isn't going to make it happen. Now's the time to do something about it. I have an idea; why not get started?"

Kimmel worked on his first book for two years, initially while living in the Virgin Islands and later while attending graduate school at the University of Illinois, where he earned a doctorate in education in 1973. Finally, he sent the finished manuscript, titled *The Tartar's Sword,* to an editor at Harper & Row who responded with a three-page critique.

"This was wonderful — the fact that an editor would take the time to read your stuff and give you suggestions — but I didn't know that because I was so green. I took it as a rejection and never even bothered to revise the book," Kimmel says.

Fortunately, instead of letting this perceived rejection stop him, Kimmel gathered courage and sent the manuscript to Coward, McCann and Geoghegan. This time, he recognized good fortune when he saw it. A top editor, Ferd Monjo, helped him revise the book for publication.

Although *The Tartar's Sword* did not become a best-seller, it drew good reviews. Kimmel received an award for it that included an invitation to a luncheon at the prestigious Lakeshore Club in Chicago. And he still remembers the thrill of running his hand over the cover bearing his name, just as he had dreamed.

After this exciting experience with his first book, Kimmel

was hooked and vowed to keep on writing. Today, he laughs at how woefully ignorant he was of the challenges awaiting him. He had proven he could get a book published, which was no small feat, but he had yet to learn what separates an eager first-time author from a seasoned professional.

### Storytelling As an Avenue for Education

From the time his first book hit the stores in 1974 until well into the 1980s, Kimmel worked doggedly at getting stories published, managing to become a regular contributor to *Cricket,* a well-respected magazine for children. This gave him a nice collection of clips to use when introducing himself to new editors and also provided a modest income while he sought to interest publishers in his books.

"I kept at it," says Kimmel. "I would have a long tough haul to get a book in print, and then it would die. A few years would go by, and I would get another in print, and it wouldn't do much. It was like pushing that rock uphill."

Meanwhile, Kimmel began networking with editors and other writers, paying close attention to career changes and business consolidations within the industry. "It's a very volatile business. People move a lot. No writer can really be associated with only one publisher, because you never really know what's going to happen tomorrow," he remarks.

Kimmel's major breakthrough came in 1988, when Margery Cuyler, a senior editor at Holiday House who looked at his story, *Hershel and the Hanukkah Goblins*, appearing in *Cricket,* said, "I want that!" Published in 1989, the book received a Caldecott Honor Medal, was selected by the National Council of Teachers of English as a Notable Children's Book, and garnered several other prestigious awards.

As a result, Holiday House asked Kimmel for more stories and continued pairing his text with artwork by excellent illustrators — an important decision that publishers traditionally reserve for themselves. Consequently, Kimmel went on to write a string of award-winning books and soon found himself in demand as a speaker. "Sometimes you can't do anything right, then all of a sudden you are hitting all over the place and you don't know why," he observes wryly.

## Practical Dreaming

Although Kimmel was already a successful author when he decided to resign his professorship at Portland State University in 1993, he nevertheless considered the move very carefully. Instead of jumping into writing full-time, he first took a sabbatical.

"I talked to an accountant. I solicited the advice of many people, because I was giving up a lot of security and a permanent, fully tenured academic position in top rank — the kind of thing people kill for. My parents were from the Depression generation, and my mother was appalled that I was contemplating giving up my job. But sometimes to get to second base and ultimately to home plate, you have to leave first base," he reflects.

Kimmel may have been following his dream, but he made sure his head was not in the clouds. He took his accountant's advice and set up a corporation to receive funds from his writing. He and his wife Doris, also a teacher, became employees of the corporation. "The advantage of this was that we were able to establish retirement programs and make sure we had medical and health benefits," says Kimmel.

Next, the company needed a name. According to Doris, "Eric thought it would be nice to have a bird name for our company name, but all we could think of were titmouse, nuthatch, crow, and vulture. Somehow those names didn't have the right ring to them. One day Eric asked me if there is a bird called shearwater. I said yes. He then asked me if I like the name, but he never asked me what the bird looked like. I told him that it has a nice sound and is not immediately associated with a bird, so we chose Shearwater as the name of our company. Weeks later, after our company was official, Eric looked the shearwater bird up in our bird book and came into my office saying, 'Doris, you didn't tell me that this bird is dull, dark, and nondescript.' 'Well,' I replied, 'you didn't ask.' So we never tell people that this bird is actually quite uninteresting!"

Without the academic work to interfere with his schedule, Kimmel had more freedom to write. However, he also faced new responsibilities, such as monitoring expenses, remaining alert to the tax implications of his activities, and deciding how best to use his time to maximize revenues — a task that proved quite challenging.

Kimmel derived his income from a variety of sources: fees for stories sold to magazines, advances on royalties for books accepted for publication, royalties from book sales, and fees and honoraria for speaking at conferences, libraries, and schools. Keeping the cash flowing, he soon realized, was a nonstop balancing act. "The dangerous thing is that you get spread too thin," Kimmel explains. "You have to make sure you are not doing too much of one thing, because then you let the others slide."

For example, speaking at schools gave Kimmel priceless feedback from children and was an important marketing activity. "Going to schools keeps your name and face in front of children who read and teachers who love books. There are a lot of books out there, and you want to give your book that special edge," he notes. But visiting too many schools exhausted him and ate away at time he needed to keep in touch with editors and publishers, do research, consider ideas, and write.

"I couldn't have done it without my wife," stresses Kimmel. "Doris wasn't teaching at the time I left the university, so this became a family business. She is the manager. She answers the telephone, arranges for plane tickets, does the scheduling and follow up."

Kimmel never considered self-publishing, although he knew several authors who were doing it and acknowledges that new technologies and processes have made self-publishing easier than ever before. "The problem with self-publishing is distribution," he explains. "Self-published books are not in the major review media, so you have to be willing to put a lot of effort into marketing. I don't want to go around the country selling copies of my book. I let publishers do that for me."

## Achieving a Fairy-Tale Ending

These days Kimmel often fields questions from people who are impressed with his critical acclaim and financial success, and yearn to follow in his footsteps. His responses reflect a blend of reality-checking and encouragement.

"You can't write because of money," he maintains. "Write because you love to do it, because in the highly competitive publishing market that may be the only reward you ever get. The thing that kept me going was a love of books and language, and telling a good story."

On the other hand, Kimmel advises people not to underestimate their chances, since persistence and practice increase the possibility of success. "Writing is a skill. The more you write, the better you get. There were always people who could write rings around me. I think the reason I became an author had nothing to do with talent. I am just the one who wanted it most," he claims.

For those considering writing as a money-making activity, Kimmel recommends "listening to people who do it, not to people who don't." He believes submitting stories to magazines is a good way to start, since such publications are often hungry for new writers.

Networking is also extremely important for writers, he adds, because they work in isolation. Kimmel networks constantly to keep abreast of what is happening in the publishing world, to receive valuable feedback about his work, and to share information on potential markets and assignments. "You meet friends along the road who really smooth the way for you," he says.

For established writers thinking of taking the plunge into entrepreneurship, Kimmel offers three fundamental observations. "First, you really need the support of your family," he says. "They can make or break you. Then you need to sit down with a competent accountant and talk about your situation, because there are all kinds of things you can do to your advantage that you would normally never know about. And you need to have courage, because it is a scary step, and you won't find out what is going to happen until you do it."

Living his dream has brought Kimmel rewards more precious than dollars. It has allowed him to pursue any interest as part of his job — from horseback riding to visiting foreign countries to learning to play video games. Recalling the day his accountant asked when he planned to retire, Kimmel says, "I don't want to retire. I think the best work you can get is work that you love. I just go out looking for stories. Every day is a new adventure."

Writing also keeps him involved in the aspect of teaching

that he loves most: contributing to the lives of young people. He shares his stories with countless youngsters at school appearances, fields their questions, gets letters from them saying they enjoyed his books, and has corresponded regularly with a number of students over the years.

But one of the best things about being an author, according to Kimmel, is that "you never know where a book goes or what it will do." A poignant anecdote illustrates his point and reveals how Kimmel measures the true value of his creations.

In 1979, Kimmel wrote a book titled *Why Worry?* that did not sell quickly. It was about two characters: one who worried all the time and another who never worried at all. To his disappointment, the book managed to stay in print only fourteen months. He had almost forgotten about it until a few years ago, when he received a letter from a children's hospital for chronic diseases frantically requesting a copy to replace one that had disappeared from their library after ten years. It turned out that the book was a favorite of young patients hospitalized for surgery or chemotherapy, because it talked about the things they were about to face.

"So even though that book didn't sell a lot of copies, was it a failure? No. Over ten years, it was doing its job, very slowly, very quietly in a corner of the world. That is success," says Kimmel.

# Chapter 12

## Diversifying Education through Cooperation

### Mounds Park Academy

*Providing a challenging academic program balanced by a sense of global responsibility and a deep commitment to the arts*

**Robert E. Kreischer, Founder**

In June 1981, Bob Kreischer left his position as a middle school director at the Breck School, a prestigious independent school in Minneapolis, Minnesota. He dedicated the ensuing year to creating a new school that would reflect Kreischer's personal vision and philosophy about children and learning. With the help of his wife, Sandy Kreischer Smith, and a small group of parents, a nonprofit coeducational college preparatory school, Mounds Park Academy (MPA), opened in 1982 with 19 staff members and 104 students, grades kindergarten to nine.

Today, MPA provides a unique education program for over 750 students in kindergarten through the twelfth grade. And now there is a waiting list for all grades.

Kreischer and the many people who believed in him succeeded in establishing precisely the type of school they envisioned. "It is exactly the size I hoped for in the beginning. It's large enough to provide the diversity I consider important in a school. But it is small enough to ensure the kind of support to the individual student necessary for a meaningful education," Kreischer comments.

The school now provides employment for over 120 full-time and part-time staff. In addition to Director Kreischer, there is a Lower School head, a Middle School head, and an Upper School head. MPA also has a full-time college counselor, a full-time dean of admissions, an athletic director, learning specialists, a full-time nurse, and several department chairpersons. The size and skills of the staff make a broad-based program a reality for all students, some of whom receive financial aid. There are multiple offerings in foreign language, music, art, drama, and physical education. Both intramural and interscholastic sports opportunities are available for middle and upper school students, and there is an extended day program for K-6. Other extracurricular opportunities include speech, debate, drama, Quiz Bowl, and Destination Imagination.

## Overcoming Limitations through Innovation

Kreischer's extensive educational background was the basis for his eventual success in making his dream a reality. He is a graduate of Macalester College in Minnesota, with a degree in psychology and history. In 1965, he moved his young family to Marin County, California, where he attended the San Francisco Theological Seminary in San Anselmo. During his three years at the seminary, Kreischer became fascinated with the field of education. As a result of his effort and enthusiasm, he was offered a fellowship to continue his studies and simultaneously earn a California teaching credential from the Dominican College of San Rafael, also in Marin County. His first year of teaching was in an innovative public middle school in Mill Valley, California. Then two years later he moved to a neighboring public school district in Tiburon, California, as a teacher, counselor, and vice principal. Within three years of earning his California administrative credential, Kreischer became the principal of the Del Mar Middle School in Tiburon.

It was in Marin County that Kreischer first experienced both the excitement and frustrations of working within the public schools. In Mill Valley and the Del Mar Middle School, Kreischer quickly learned the limitations as well as the opportunities afforded a creative administrator and staff when planning and providing educational opportunities. He soon realized that teaching strategies or classroom programs that were particularly effective for some students were often inappropriate for others, especially when individual families' goals and values were taken into account. Thus, Kreischer learned the dilemma facing many dedicated educators: how to initiate change to help some students without simultaneously hindering others.

In the late 1970s, a family tragedy made it necessary for Kreischer to return to Minnesota with his family. At that time both administrative and teaching jobs were very difficult to find, and as a result Kreischer accepted his first teaching job in an independent school, the Breck School. For one year he taught English, mathematics, and science in grades six, seven, and eight. In the second year, Kreischer was appointed middle school director and was responsible for overseeing budgets, admissions, and curriculum for grades five to eight. He recalls, "During the two years I did that, I found that I had some pretty major disagreements with the headmaster of the school. The longer those disagreements lasted, the more uncomfortable I became. By the end of my second year as middle school head, I decided that if I felt so strongly about what I believed, it was only ethical that I resign, and resign I did. I was pretty turned off to education at that time. It seemed that what I wanted to do with kids and learning was next to impossible in both public and independent schools. Of course looking back, it is immediately obvious that my experiences were pretty much limited to two public schools and one independent one in less than ten years — hardly enough exposure to make a life-wrenching decision. Yet I decided that I had to do something else."

Kreischer was not certain what else he wanted to do until a friend, knowing of Kreischer's previous interest in starting a school, reminded him of his earlier statements. Kreischer recalls, "My wife and a friend, who also taught at Breck, were sitting around during the summer, and she said, 'You know, you should start a school. You have been talking about that for a long time.' She was right. I talked about it even when I was in California. My wife, Sandy, joined in and supported the idea. I wasn't too excited. I didn't have the slightest idea of how to do something like that. We began talking with others. Much of the research was done by Sandy. She called independent schools throughout the state — and even as far away as Chicago, to the Independent Schools Association of the Central States (ISACS). Together we decided that if we were going to move forward, we had to be incorporated. The first step in that process was the establishment of a board."

Based on what information Kreischer had learned by calling others and reading, he and his wife decided that the best way to organize was as a nonprofit entity. At Breck School he had learned the importance of being accredited, and he wanted any school he started to be immediately considered for accreditation. ISACS, the regional independent arm of NAIS, was able to accredit the school early on, as well as NES, the organization accrediting public schools in Minnesota.

## Uniting for Common Objectives

In refining his vision for the new school, Kreischer developed a commitment to both a strong academic program and cooperation between all factions in the school. As Kreischer sums up the views at the time: "The first thing we had to do was to get the support of a group of people who shared our vision. That vision became clearer every day. We knew that eventually we wanted a small school of no more than 750 to 800 students. We wanted to have students from kindergarten through high school. We wanted a place where five year olds would learn side by side with seventeen and eighteen year olds. We wanted a strong academic, liberal arts program that would lead to successful college and university experiences. We wanted a school that had a commitment to community service and diversity. We wanted to create a learning environment that would support professional teachers and help them grow. We wanted a school where the emphasis was on 'together we,' not 'I,' 'me,' 'they,' or even 'we.' We wanted to support an all-inclusive process involving students, teachers, parents, administrators, and the board working together for common objectives."

Even after the decision had been made about the type of school desired and how to organize it, the vision did not immediately become a reality. For almost a year there was no building, no staff, no equipment, no supplies or materials — but only commitment to a particular educational philosophy that had been established jointly by Kreischer and the newly formed board of about a dozen people. The philosophy became immediately recognizable not only in what Kreischer and the board said, but in how they went about translating those ideas into daily interactions. This cooperation between participants concretely reflected the envisioned philosophy of "together we."

Kreischer comments on the time: "We literally started with about fifteen hundred dollars. We decided to use most of that to see if there was any interest in our ideas. We advertised a couple of informational meetings. While doing that, we were looking at several possible buildings and beginning our search for good, experienced teachers. The good news was that at this time enrollments were dropping in the public school sector. Some public schools were closing, and outstanding teachers with many years of experience were being let go. We constantly talked about our school. We were not deceiving anyone. Obviously the school didn't exist. We talked about what *could* be, what *would* be. Even in these first descriptive meetings we had applications, which was most encouraging."

Fortunately, Kreischer and his supporters found an existing school building on a site that could be renovated to meet the requirements of the new school they envisioned. This enabled them to open the school without further delay. Originally the buildings were designed to house a public school of between 700 and 800 students. The classrooms were traditional. There was nothing artistic or inviting about the school's design or layout, but it was a godsend. A board member had heard about the local district's interest in leasing the facility, and eventually the district and the Mounds Park Academy (MPA) board agreed on a contract that allowed MPA to lease not only the building but most of the desks and equipment as well. The existing 15,000-volume library was purchased outright. So by September 1982, there was a school ready to offer the educational program originally promised. Within two years, the district decided to sell instead of lease, which was fortunate for MPA. Through the efforts of many people, the use of promissory notes, and fund drives that secured donations from parents and interested community members, the multiacre site was purchased by the school. In its third year, Mounds Park Academy became a self-sufficient educational operation.

During the 1981 to 1982 school year, Kreischer devoted all of his energy to establishing the school. By maintaining her career as a successful potter, his wife provided the money needed to keep the family afloat while Kreischer and an increasing number of potential parents, interested teachers, and community members made plans for the school. Kreischer recalls how even in the first year growth exceeded expectations: "At first we wanted to start with a K-9 school of about 180 kids. While talking with a representative from the ISACS, we were told to keep the enrollment to 30 or 40 students, that it would be impossible to find 180 the first year. We compromised and set our goal at 120. To make a long story short, we opened our doors with 104 students and ended that year with 111. The next year we had 236, and there has been steady growth since. Looking back, I'd say that the ISACS guy wasn't too far off. I know of two other schools started within a year of us that had 30 to 40 kids at first."

## Maintaining a Vision of Teamwork

When visiting MPA today, it is almost impossible to envision the original building or site, since several remodeling and building projects have resulted in a very modern and aesthetically pleasing educational facility complete with new playing fields, a large gymnasium, an impressive theater complex, parking areas, tennis courts, and computer laboratories. The vision of the school as a place of cooperation between various groups has been maintained. In some of the corridors, high school and middle school students study in classrooms next to primary-level students. Art, writing, and other examples of student work line the walls of classrooms and corridors. In keeping with the "together we" vision, every school year a concept is selected as a focus for study and reflection by all students regardless of age. For example, last year that concept was family while this year it is diversity. The close relationships between older and younger students, reinforced through a program of "buddies," creates a sense of family and mutual support.

Throughout the school there is a feeling of belonging and

pride. Cabinets displaying a wide variety of honors earned by MPA students are in evidence everywhere. Besides team and individual sport awards in such diverse activities as soccer, basketball, golf, and tennis, there are cups and trophies for excellence in music, drama, poetry, creative writing, and other academic areas. In addition, there are plaques celebrating outstanding teachers of the year in foreign language, science, soccer, and art. Certificates indicating recognition by the US Department of Education, the Children's Theatre Foundation of America, the Minnesota Academic Excellence League, and the Governor's Star Award Program are also in evidence. All in all, one immediately senses that MPA is a school with a strong vision and success in filling its mission.

Kreischer takes great pride in the accomplishments of the past seventeen years, not the least of which is the fact that 100 percent of the academy's graduates have been admitted to a college or university. Another point of satisfaction for Kreischer is both the quality and small turnover of the staff. This is because of the many things done to enhance the professionalism and satisfaction of teachers, including a careful selection process, a good evaluation program, and a unique salary system paying everyone the same after three years' experience at the school, a program of zero-based budgeting that allows the teacher to be in control of classroom materials, adequate preparation time, access to secretarial services, payment for courses and workshops selected by teachers, mini-sabbaticals, and other institutionalized procedures that support the "together we" vision.

While the school has ultimately been very successful, Kreischer has had to overcome several obstacles along the way. Some of the challenges have been determining how to handle transportation and lunch programs, providing scholarships for deserving students, ensuring a diverse student population, and assuring adequate finances to pay salaries appropriate for teachers who have been employed at MPA for close to twenty years.

Yet, to Kreischer, having had the opportunity to realize a dream and effect a positive change in education has been extremely worthwhile despite any challenges he has faced. He sums up his experiences in the following way: "I haven't really had the time to reflect on all that has happened, but I can tell you that when I talk with graduates, parents, staff members, and current students, I know that we made the right decision. Every moment of worry, every gray hair, and you can see there are many, are worth it. And possibly the most exciting thing is that we are never done. I think making a dream come alive, even one that is at first very hazy, and living that dream is a high level of achievement. Yes, it takes energy and commitment and lots of help, but as far as I can see, the effort is justified and worthy of any sacrifice I might have made financially in terms of job security. I would encourage anyone thinking of striking out on their own to try it — to adopt a 'can do' spirit. The worst thing that can happen is that you might fail; but in the long run, doing something you no longer enjoy can be evidence of even greater failure."

# Chapter 13

## Providing Visual Resources for Educators

### The LPD Video Journal of Education, Inc.

*Exciting in-service programs to support and improve teaching*

**Blanch and John Linton, Cofounders**

The exterior of the building housing The LPD Video Journal of Education, Inc., located in Sandy, Utah, is not particularly impressive. A regular office building shared with an insurance agency gives the visitor's vision of an average small business operation that produces professional development videotapes for educators. However, upon entering the building, this impression is immediately changed and enhanced. The people actively engaged in what they are doing, the openness of the areas, the artwork, and the various awards the company has received make the visitor aware that this is a vibrant, strong, and exciting business. This feeling becomes even stronger upon meeting Blanch and John Linton, partners in business and partners in life.

Today, the Video Journal produces six or seven volumes of in-service videotapes per year. Each volume contains two, three, or four programs with suggestions for use and focuses on a particular topic or issue of importance to districts, schools, and teachers. A recognized professional, one who has contributed to the research and classroom application of that particular issue, is contracted to present the core. The words, examples, and visual aids used by the presenter are enhanced by samples of actual classroom applications by real teachers and students. Thus teachers who view the tapes can quickly see how the ideas can be used in their classrooms.

Presenters come from a variety of sources. Some are university professors, researchers, or administrators; many are classroom teachers; and some are professional consultants. All have at least two things in common: they are accomplished, exciting presenters or workshop leaders, and they have access to the real world where their ideas and practical strategies are being implemented. It is this combination of theory and practice that makes the work of the Video Journal particularly valuable.

The Video Journal is a very successful enterprise, having sold well over 30,000 volumes, or upward of 180,000 individual tapes. Schools and districts in every state have purchased them, as well as schools in all other English-speaking countries. They are also popular in several countries where English is not the official language. A wide range of issues is covered on the tapes including classroom management, individualized instruction, the use of technology in the classroom, critical thinking, cooperative learning, reading, mathematics, and creativity.

## Educating through Heart and Brain

The Lintons could not foresee the future when John, a classroom teacher in Utah's Jordin School District, was asked to produce some in-service videotapes for the district. The district was aware that John had worked as a cameraman, director, and producer before becoming a teacher. John accepted the offer to develop videos on topics such as the work of Dr. William Glasser, lesson planning, classroom control, and reporting to parents. The district also assigned Blanch, a successful teacher, to assist her husband in this stimulating program. Both John and Blanch had attended in-service meetings and had firsthand knowledge of the less than successful attempts at using films and videotapes to help teachers. Consequently, they realized it was important to produce something significantly different. Blanch recalls, "John was and is a very creative producer. We both had sat through many educational tapes and films that were dull and boring. We knew what teachers did when these were showing — correct papers, write lesson plans, write letters, and pay bills. We decided to make interesting and artistic programs that would reach people emotionally. We wanted to produce films with high entertainment value that would keep interest high."

John and Blanch realized that to be interesting, their films had to incorporate music, animation, rich narration, and above all, great pictures of kids and real classroom practices. They had to make their videos emotional. John feels that most teachers are emotional people who care: "They are attracted to the profession because of their hearts as well as their brains. They see a lot of affective value in what they do." Both Blanch and John consider the concepts of emotion and entertainment significant to the presentation of material. They work diligently at preserving the integrity of ideas while simultaneously respecting the time and energy of their audience.

The high quality of the work produced by John and Blanch eventually attracted the attention of people throughout the neighboring areas and eventually the state as well. Soon they were asked to do video productions for private companies and other public agencies, making it impossible for the Lintons to keep their regular jobs in the district. As a result, like many other entrepreneurs they resigned from their jobs, took out their retirement monies, bought some basic equipment, and created their own business. John explains: "We started as a partnership with three other people. They liked the idea of the Video Journal and they also liked the idea of developing commercial programs for private businesses. These people put some seed money into the partnership. Very soon after the company started, conflicts came up. The investors saw the company as a cash cow, a way to make a lot of money. They wanted the profits returned in the form of dividends. We wanted to use the money to grow the company. Our vision was to put the profits into the company so we could do a better job. We were more interested in teaching and learning than we were in developing commercials and infomercials. Eventually, we ended up in control of the company, and we were able to see it grow in the direction we wanted."

Today, the Video Journal is housed in a building that provides space for Blanch and John, as well as for dozens of writers, camerapeople, computer technicians, sales consultants, packagers, and other warehouse staff. There is a small studio and editing area furnished with equipment such as cameras, computers, editing machines, and a variety of recording devices. In addition, the lower floor contains over 5,000 square feet of warehouse space. The ample facilities are in striking contrast to the first location of the Video Journal — the family living room, dining room, and garage.

### Encouraging Honest Communication

The Video Journal, like other companies developed by educational entrepreneurs for the improvement of learning, provides quality products for its clients. However, what makes this business different from many others is the relationship that exists between the two principals. Both Blanch and John were involved in the projects that formed the foundation for the company — producing programs on Dr. William Glasser's control theory, learning, and human needs; building relationships among school staffs; collegiality, site-based management, and the empowering of people; and honest communication. Their experiences creating such programs played a part not only in the evolution of the company but also in the development of the open, trusting, supportive, and loving relationship John and Blanch share.

John knows that Blanch is better at the nitty-gritty everyday work of the company. She worries about the finances. She makes the contacts, and reviews the scripts. John remarks, "It defies the typical male-female role models. She is the driving force behind getting the job done. My expertise is on the creative side of it. If I gave her a camera, she would mess it up."

Blanch replies, "And I wouldn't want it. I have no desire to create or direct. I'm in on the production in the role of producer. John is the artistic one. Together we make a great team."

Moreover, the Lintons carry over their personal learning to all of their associations with clients, presenters, and staff. They are especially aware of how their respect for others influences their behavior with the staff. The Video Journal relies heavily on the loyalty of all its employees, including three of the couple's children. Actually, all five of their children have made important contributions to the success of the Video Journal. One of their sons is vice president in charge of marketing, and his wife is the financial manager. Another son writes, and the youngest son does data entry. A fourth son, who now works for Microsoft, set up the database and met his wife when she was in sales for the journal. A daughter, currently living in Thailand, continues to do the proofreading for the company. All printed materials are faxed to her prior to final approval.

John and Blanch are very appreciative of family members and staff who have been instrumental in making the business successful. Blanch states: "We recognize how dependent we are for our past successes as well as our future. The same ideas we use to maintain communication and trust between the two of us, we use with the staff. We really try to walk the talk of what we are all about. We offer a good benefits plan, as well as a profit-sharing plan. We have had to learn all aspects of running a business and having employees. It has been an incredible and complex learning experience. We have excellent people working with us and wonderful people to help along the way. We have been very fortunate."

### Emphasizing the Importance of Teachers

It is evident that the Lintons's success in business is due in large part to their continued passion about their mission, which is "to improve the quality of today's schools," and their focus on producing quality products. Blanch says, "We want to make sure everything we present has the proven capacity to improve learning. Our mission is to enhance teaching and learning in the schools. It is very simple — John and I talk about it constantly with each other and with our employees. We are passionate about our mission."

To maintain quality control and customer satisfaction, the Lintons solicit comments from all their users. Besides the regular evaluations of videos already produced, to determine future productions they send out surveys to their clients, do a great deal of reading, attend conferences, and consult with teachers, community representatives, and administrators. They realize that while they use computer technology, up-to-date editing equipment, and the Internet in making their videotapes, they are not a videotape or a technology company but rather an information production company that regards videotape as merely a medium of delivery. Selecting topics and presenters for the tapes are the most important decisions to be made each year. Once those decisions are made in house, the focus shifts to quality.

Production quality is a constant, as is the immediate and practical application of the ideas to classroom situations. No presenters are used unless they are able to provide access to real schools, classrooms, and children. Everything the Video Journal produces is both thoroughly researched and tested in classrooms. In addition, considerable attention is paid to the entertainment value and emotional impact of productions. John explains, "We try to write narration and select music that emphasizes the importance teachers have in society. When we talk about children, we are speaking of the future of the world. When we talk about teachers, we know we are talking about real people who have feelings of joy and pain. We have a high regard for teachers and students. This is powerful stuff. Maintaining quality takes constant vigilance." As a result of these considerations, every production is evidence that the Video Journal takes its mission seriously.

Like all entrepreneurs, the Lintons are aware of their current strengths as well as changes occurring around them. They know they are operating an information production company, and they know that videotape is an effective and affective delivery system; in fact, the programs are now being videostreamed on the interactive Internet site *www.TeachStream.com.* At the same time, the Lintons are open to the idea of using a different medium and are currently planning the use of CD-ROM. They are partnering with someone who produces DVD players and offering the player and disk in one package. Earlier, they considered going into business with vendors who were trying to put together a package deal to sell programs to satellite facilities. John states, "There is always something on the horizon, but you are never sure. Making changes is risky. Videotape is our bread and butter. We have to think and experiment, but if we don't keep up the basic fabric of our business, we'll go flat."

Both Blanch and John recognize that willingness to take risks is an essential trait for any potential entrepreneur. They believe that taking that first step is a huge stumbling block for many interested in becoming more independent. As Blanch says, "You have to do a lot of research. You have to do your homework. There are a lot of decisions involved. There is a lot to think about." John adds, "I think people have to be ready to sacrifice. You have to be willing to go without a paycheck. We lived tight for a long time. We made a big sacrifice; in fact, our whole family made sacrifices at first. But it has been worth it."

As for personal satisfaction, John and Blanch are constantly rewarded by teachers who tell them how much the programs have influenced their lives. They know that they have an important role in helping teachers grow and in improving education. They know that for them, becoming entrepreneurs was the right decision.

John stresses that whenever a person makes an important decision, they should reflect on everything they believe, think, value, and aspire to. He says, "Deciding to leave the classroom is a very big and personal decision. Some teachers are happy in the classroom. Others say that although they are happy, they want something different. Everyone has to follow the path that leads to satisfaction. Not everyone should be a teacher. Not everyone should be a businessperson. One must do what brings personal rewards. That goes right to integrity. If you really want to do something you're not doing, you are out of alignment."

Blanch adds, "I think it is critical for people to be passionate about what they are doing. We have a lot of passion about the Video Journal. Teachers who are successful are very passionate about what they are doing. It seems passion is a driving and energizing force for anything we do well."

The Lintons not only walk their talk; they also radiate it. After only a minute with them, one cannot help but feel their passion, their commitment, and their integrity.

# Chapter 14

## Expanding Education through Global Learning

### Educational Field Studies, Inc.

*A student travel company*

**Larry Lusvardi, Founder**

In 1968, Larry Lusvardi, a successful high school social studies teacher and football coach in southern California, was able to parlay two compelling and compatible interests, teaching and travel, into an exciting business. From personal experience he knew the power of direct experiential learning. Books, films, records, and speakers were certainly good sources of information when studying about another culture in the classroom. Similarly, maps, globes, models, and pictures could help his students develop a sense of geography. But Lusvardi believed that real learning and understanding best came from direct experience. As a social science major, he recognized the importance of primary sources for research. He also knew that travel gave students a chance to learn about such things as following schedules, using money appropriately, and living in close quarters with nonfamily members over an extended period of time. Further, he was aware that it presented opportunities to develop insights into such psychological concepts as motivation, group behavior, problem solving, and decision making.

As a coach, Lusvardi knew the importance of teamwork and cooperation, and understood that successful travel with a group of students depends on those concepts. In addition, such travel would give Lusvardi himself opportunity to continue his personal journey of learning about history, geography, economics, philosophy, and anthropology. After careful consideration, it was clear to him that a well-planned trip to another part of the world would be the best way to help students develop a thorough comprehension of another culture while instilling many humanistic values.

## Learning Opportunities through Travel

In the late 1950s Lusvardi began his teaching and coaching career in southern California. After a few years of teaching, a feeling of wanderlust prompted him to apply for a position with the United States Department of Defense Schools in Europe. He was accepted and assigned to a school in Germany. During his two-year stay, from 1965 to 1967, Lusvardi and his family traveled extensively throughout central Europe. Each weekend and holiday provided an opportunity to explore areas about which he was teaching, intensifying his interest in the people, history, and customs observed throughout the continent. But for a variety of reasons such as tenure, retirement programs, and the needs of his family, it was time to return to California and resume his teaching and coaching responsibilities.

After returning home, Lusvardi realized that he had two things he could market. He knew teaching, and he knew how to travel inexpensively in Europe. He had learned that travel could be both exhilarating and educational, and he wanted to help students feel that same excitement in European cities, museums, and monuments. Further, he wished to help young people develop the kind of understanding and appreciation he had for other cultures, languages, and people. He had an intense desire to open the eyes of young people to the world about them, and in a such a way that he could also enrich his own life without getting into debt. Consequently, he established Educational Field Studies, Inc.

In the summer of 1968, the new company offered its first

student travel experience. Lusvardi organized a camping trip to Europe for nineteen of his high school students. The excitement those first students felt upon their return was quickly transmitted to others, and in 1969 Lusvardi arranged another trip, this time with over double the number of students and additional adults. During the next several years, the operation expanded with other teachers and counselors spreading the word throughout their schools. While on the one hand having more and more students sign up each year made the operation more successful, on the other hand the numbers made logistics more difficult. Lusvardi was never sure of the final number of student participants until very near the day of travel, when the deadline for registration had passed. Only then were the additional teachers and counselors hired, airplane tickets ordered, and Volkswagen buses purchased.

Lusvardi had discovered that he could purchase buses in Germany and sell them upon his return to California, a plan that added to the growing success of his business. Later, however, when the costs involved with bringing used Volkswagen buses back to the United States for sale made that activity financially prohibitive, he had to change tactics. Soliciting the help of an automobile dealer in Holland solved the problem. Lusvardi recalls, "I worked with a guy in Amsterdam. We would buy used buses, drive them around Europe all summer, and sell them back to him. We had a great understanding. I would visit him in the morning. He would offer me a beer. I would tell him how many buses I would need. I would look around his stock, pick out those I wanted, and at the same time point out what changes I needed in the number and placement of seats. He would take notes and say, 'Go to lunch.' I would come back in a couple of hours and there they were, just as I had ordered. They were all gassed up, clean as a whistle, and ready to roll. It was amazing."

Another challenge for Lusvardi was operating Educational Field Studies (EFS) on an unpredictable budget. Each year, as the number of participants, teachers, and counselors grew, planning became more difficult and time-consuming. Lusvardi had to juggle financial factors while simultaneously teaching and coaching. Soon the necessity of preparing for both his school and travel responsibilities began to create conflict and stress.

## Cross-Cultural Perspectives

The early 1970s was a pivotal period for Lusvardi's growing business. In 1973, EFS was incorporated under the laws of California. In 1974, Lusvardi married Carla, his former student-teacher and trip leader whom he hired in 1972. Then in 1974, EFS established contracts with the ABC School District in southern California to carry out their field trip programs throughout the school year. The assistant superintendent of that district knew of Lusvardi's success in Europe and of his interest in expanding the offerings of EFS. Consequently, he suggested that Lusvardi come to his district to work as an independent contractor organizing field trips for the district, as he believed in the educational benefits of such experiences. Says Lusvardi, "He figured that if I could coordinate those various trips, I could help him, the district, and especially the kids. As an independent contractor, all the district had to do was provide me with an office and pay my fee. No tenure. No benefits. No long-term commitment from either of us."

It was then that Larry and Carla knew they had to make a decision about whether or not to operate EFS full-time and quit their teaching jobs. Ultimately, they both resigned their classroom responsibilities to devote their energies to their new educational careers as organizers of exciting educational travel experiences for students.

By 1976 two other districts, Alta Loma District and the Inglewood Unified District, had contracted with EFS for all the educational field trips offered in addition to establishing an adult school educational program, which became part of EFS's total package. This not only generated state money, but it added to the educational value of the trip as well. The money collected through the state's Average Daily Attendance (ADA) formula was used to help pay for the programs and help subsidize the expenses of individual students.

As a result, the company grew in size and stature. More and more districts contracted with the company, and full-time staff was added. By this time most of the company's income derived from the state through the districts instead of through individual families. Districts were receiving educational benefits for their students without providing staff. They had control over the quality and quantity of the trips without incurring many direct or indirect costs associated with organizing and administrating educational travel programs.

## Downsizing and Rebuilding

Then in 1978, the funding structure for all California public schools was drastically changed. California's famous tax reform initiative, Proposition 13, that had been approved by voters in 1977, became effective in 1978. In response, the schools had to drop many services and programs including the field trips organized by EFS. This had a very negative impact on the business. As Lusvardi explains, "Overnight, the primary source of our funding was gone. Carla and I had to make a serious decision, and make it quickly. We had learned to love what we were doing. We knew we were good at it. So, we decided to take a chance. We had to let go of nearly all our staff. We sold our home in Huntington Harbor. We sold the nicest of our two cars. We moved into an apartment with little or no furniture. We moved the office into that apartment. It was either shift gears and try to rebuild — that is, go back to the drawing board — or return to teaching. We both loved teaching, but we had learned to love our business even more. So we went out in search of new markets. We found the independent schools, and we found the individual families. We began learning how to sell our product. We started offering trips from southern California to Sacramento, our state capital, and continued our summer trips to Europe. Together those trips became the backbone of our new start."

Like many entrepreneurs, the Lusvardis found that when confronted with a serious problem, basically two alternatives are available — to give up or to regroup and continue. The Lusvardis opted to keep their business and look for ways to develop it further.

After making the commitment to stay in business, the Lusvardis decided to branch out. Soon they were offering students from throughout California, Nevada, Oregon, and Washington trips to Washington, DC; Cape Canaveral, Florida; Historic Virginia; Massachusetts; and summer camps in Hawaii. Working with the Disneyland Hotel in Anaheim, EFS was the first to offer "Grad Nights" at Disneyland to students from other states. They worked with Disneyland to establish "Magic Music Days," for which EFS brought choral and band groups to perform at the hotel or at Disneyland itself. Under the Lusvardis' leadership, the University of Southern California Music Department came to critique and advise these performing groups — another good example of EFS's emphasis on education as part of travel opportunities.

## Education for the Age of Global Awareness

Currently, an increasing number of California public schools has learned how to budget for the important learning experiences EFS offers. As a result of additional demand for its services, EFS has increased the number of offices and expanded its offerings. Today, EFS has four offices — the main office in Incline Village, Nevada, and other offices in Orange County, California, Washington, DC, and Orlando, Florida. During the 1998 to 1999 school year, EFS provided travel opportunities to over 50,000 students, a number that reflects its consistent 10 percent yearly growth rate for the past several years. EFS now offers trips to such diverse locations as Philadelphia, Gettysburg, Walt Disney World's EPCOT Center, and Pearl Harbor, Hawaii, and focuses on such diverse topics as history, science, and music. Each trip is augmented by a teacher's curriculum guide that provides background information as well as suggestions for "Discovery Activities" for both before and after travel. Students also receive their own "Discovery Guide," which presents information and includes space for recording experiences and insights during the trip. It is because of this conscientious planning and follow-up that EFS is currently the only fully accredited student travel company in the United States, having been accredited by the Northwest Association of Schools and Colleges in 1997.

Despite the growth of EFS, the Lusvardis are still the principal stockholders and remain active on the board of directors. The chief executive officer is Ron DeCaprio, while the president is Lusvardi's nephew Mark Lusvardi — both of whom are former student travelers and have been active in the company in some capacity since its inception.

The company's most recent development has been the establishment of the Learning Center Discovery Laboratory, a foundation dedicated to the training of teachers to meet the challenges of education in the twenty-first century. This exciting new concept is housed in a magnificent two-story building in Incline Village. There state-of-the-art communication and technological equipment make it possible for the Learning Center Foundation to provide hands-on, two-way training sessions in the use of technology to teachers and administrators simultaneously throughout the world.

### Building Relationships

To ensure future growth of EFS, Lusvardi recognized the importance of establishing and maintaining good relationships with his contacts. He comments, "The positive relationships we established with people in Europe many years ago made it possible to do business even though we were separated by thousands of miles. Relationships of trust and cooperation with management from the airlines, hotels, tourist sites, school districts, and land transportation companies make it possible for us to build new programs at the same time we maintain and refine the old. We are in the people business."

It is evident that the Lusvardis value trust, respect, and comradeship in relationships with their staff as well as with their clients. They obviously care not only about their product but about the people who help deliver it. Each of their approximately 110 full-time and 550 part-time trip counselors is constantly screened, reviewed, and supported. Each, regardless of previous experience, is trained to ensure that there is complete understanding of the mission and goals of the company.

Probably the most important relationship of all is the one shared by the Lusvardis themselves. Larry and Carla have been married for over twenty-five years. They ski together, golf together, and work together. Larry says without hesitation that this is one of the elements essential to his success as an entrepreneur.

When asked about rewards he has received from his many years in education — first as a teacher and football coach, and then as a travel organizer — Lusvardi smiles and replies with a twinkle in his eye: "You know, I taught a lot of kids in fifteen years. And whenever I'm lucky enough to see one of them now, they say, 'Remember the field trips we took?' They never say, 'That was sure a great lecture you gave.'"

Thus, the Lusvardis have had a very positive experience being entrepreneurs in the field of education. Although in December 1999 they sold EFS to Lakeland Holdings, they still retain an interest in the Learning Center Discovery Laboratory and take great pride in their overall accomplishments in helping students learn through the excitement of travel.

# Chapter 15

## Fostering Understanding in the Education Industry

### The Education Industry Group, LLC

*Providing information on the growing education industry*

**Dr. John M. McLaughlin, Founder**

When it comes to education, there are many bottom lines. Certainly test scores, parent satisfaction, drop-out rates, program offerings, teachers' salaries, administrative duties, scholarship possibilities, and teacher-pupil ratios are among them. And as John McLaughlin points out in his publication, *The Education Industry Report®*, so, too, is the notion of profit. McLaughlin, while certainly not the first to realize that education is one of the biggest businesses in the United States, is currently a leader in helping others see that profit is an increasingly acceptable bottom line in education. This is something book publishers, film producers, architects, suppliers, authors, university professors, and educational consultants have known for years since such groups have all benefited from the multibillion-dollar business of education.

McLaughlin's *Education Industry Report* was established to provide information on this growing industry. It focuses on six sectors: educational management, educational products, educational service organizations, at-risk youth, post-secondary education, and training and development. EIR also includes The EI Index®, a Dow Jones-like average for the education industry. EI Index tracks thirty publicly traded education companies on a monthly basis. While not offered for investment advice, The EI Index serves as a barometer of the education industry's performance.

In addition to The El Index, which McLaughlin developed, EIR also features articles by various leaders from education, business, and industry, as well as profiles of diverse people whose contributions have been newsworthy. Christopher Cross, president and CEO of the Council for Basic Education, Mark Myers, superintendent of Duluth Public Schools, Paul Hill, director of Re-Inventing Public Education, Gary Beckner, executive director of the Association of American Educators, Arthur Levine, president of Columbia Teachers' College, and both Milton and Rose Friedman have all been profiled. Included too are legislative updates, commentaries, news items, a market analysis, and a section called Company Focus.

The Education Industry Group (EIG) also has a consulting arm whose aim is to help people translate information into action. McLaughlin sees it as "a bridge between the investor, corporate, government, and education communities." Some EIG clients are considering entering the educational arena. Others are searching for ways to expand their services. McLaughlin is especially excited about the work EIG does with investment firms eager to learn more about opportunities in the education industry. Through a part of the business McLaughlin refers to as "venture design," he helps startup companies in the industry and is paid with ownership in the new endeavor. EIG has consulted with local and state agencies attempting to create more efficient education delivery systems and has also worked with such diverse groups as the National School Boards Association and the World Bank.

## Finding Fulfillment through Independence

The story behind McLauglin's career decisions should be of particular interest to entrepreneurs. McLaughlin's father was a product of his time. He grew up during the Depression, was a

World War II veteran, went to work in corporate America, and became very successful working for a Fortune 50 company. While he enjoyed all the benefits of success in life, he also believed something was missing. He lacked independence. He thought that the best way to find happiness was to be his own boss, a belief he passed on to his son. McLaughlin says, "My father was convinced that even if you are a person of modest means, as long as you are independent you have the best chance for real happiness. My father thought that independence was something of great value. Business success, advancing through the company, operating through a chain of command — my father hated that. The idea of independence was instilled in my soul."

This background, coupled with McLaughlin's "miserable high school experience," in some seemingly strange way strongly influenced his choice of a profession. He recalls, "I think part of my decision was just plain defiance. I was a believer in education. I saw it as a great equalizer. I believed that education would help us achieve desegregation, peace in our time, and economic equality. I thought public education would do all of that. I wanted to make a difference. I felt that being a teacher was antiestablishment. We were in Vietnam. The thought of getting a business degree or becoming an engineer and joining the military-industrial machine was abhorrent to me. Even though that machine, through my father, had given me an extremely good life, I felt that I had to do something different. My father just couldn't understand how I was going to make a living as a teacher. He said, 'Be independent. Don't be a teacher.' But I was a young Turk who believed every liberal idea fed me. I was going to make a difference."

McLaughlin graduated with a teaching certificate in geography from George Peabody College in 1974, and after completing a master's degree program at the University of Chicago, he returned to Nashville to work with special education students in a small independent elementary school. He explains, "I loved working with those bright kids. They needed a lot of individual support. They were exciting to work with. Each one had so much to give. But it became evident that in Nashville there was no appropriate high school for them after they left our school."

## Advocating Effective Educational Change

At the age of twenty-four, with only two years' experience, McLaughlin took his first bold step toward becoming an entrepreneur in education. In 1977, with $3,000 borrowed from a local bank, he established the nonprofit Benton Hall High School, named after the famous artist Thomas Hart Benton. The facility was not designed as a four-year school but as an institution for intensive individualized learning opportunities that would allow students to be successful in a standard high school after six months to a year or two at Benton Hall. The school began with only one student, and by the end of its first year there were eleven.

In 1979, the school received accreditation, and after twenty-three years the school is still in existence. There are many reasons why the school, which eventually purchased and renovated a closed public school, not only survived but grew. First, it has always offered a quality program designed to meet individual needs of students. Second, it meshes well with the music industry so important in Nashville. Today, one of McLaughlin's major tasks in his capacity as board member is fund-raising. Through his and other people's efforts, the school has benefited from fund-raising concerts presented by such luminaries as Waylon Jennings, John Prine, Emmy Lou Harris, the Indigo Girls, Riders in the Sky, and Michael McDonald from the Doobie Brothers.

## Profit versus Nonprofit

Four years after McLaughlin established Benton Hall High School, he began to consider changing its status to a for-profit venture. He comments, "Around 1981 or so I thought, 'Why not make the school for profit?' I had my name on the line. I was borrowing money against my home, yet I could only get salary. If we made $100,000 in one year, which we never did, it would all go back into the school. Maybe I could get a $5,000 bonus. My brother, one of the best child psychologists in Nashville was on the board for years. He never drew a dime from it. And the IRS audits were horrendous. So, I asked my lawyer what we could do to make it a for-profit corporation. The procedure was just too difficult. Besides, I thought I would have to give up my accreditation. This was before I had heard of the National Independent Private Schools Association (NIPSA), which is an accrediting organization for deserving independent schools for profit."

In addition to financial considerations, one of the reasons for considering the change in the school status was to gain greater independence — the value McLaughlin's father had instilled in him. Another reason was to transfer the model he had developed to other locations. McLaughlin saw that there was an opportunity to influence education on a much wider scale.

However, that dream did not materialize since, in 1985, after recognizing that he was getting tired of "working in the trenches," McLaughlin asked the Benton Hall board for a sabbatical to pursue a PhD. He remembers, "I went to the University of Minnesota to work on a doctorate. I did the fastest PhD program in the universe. Minnesota was a great school. It allowed me to transfer many credits and write my dissertation in absentia. It was on the role of the private sector in education."

It was while McLaughlin was living in St. Paul that many things came into focus. He met a friend whose relative was one of the greatest venture capitalists in the country, Jack Massey. Massey's firm showed McLaughlin a vision of the future of American education that excited him. As a result of this interaction, McLaughlin gained increasing respect for the free market. As he reveals: "It showed me that the people who were going to change education were not in the Superintendent's Association, the School Board Association, or even in the Parent Teacher Association. Instead, it would come from people who brought in capital, vision, technology, accountability, and a demand for quality. They would be the change agents."

## A Quest for Change

Also while attending the University of Minnesota, McLaughlin met Julie Remund, the woman he was to marry. She was studying medicine and in residence for her degree. After their marriage, McLaughlin commuted between St. Paul and Nashville although he was always conscientious about making sure Benton Hall School was running efficiently regardless of his absence.

In 1987, the McLaughlin family moved to St. Cloud, Minnesota, where Julie McLaughlin joined a private medical practice and John became a professor at St. Cloud State University. He states, "I taught in the Administrators Licensing Program. I taught school law, which was pretty useful for what I ended up doing. Like the new teacher at a high school, I ended up teaching all kinds of subjects. My research was on the private sector. I became a part-time consultant with the Economic Council of America. This opened up all kinds of doors for me. I was soon speaking and writing for such diverse groups as the National School Boards Association, the Forum of Educational Leaders, the National Catholic Schools Association, and the Association of School Superintendents."

Even though McLaughlin was gaining useful knowledge, experience, and contacts, he had a growing sense that he was not contributing to change in education in a meaningful way. It was at this time that he first published *The Education Investor*, the precursor of the *Education Industry Report*. He recalls, "I found that for me, being a professor in higher education was one of the poorest ways of making an effective change in the lives of kids. I felt distanced from kids, but worse than that I felt I was part of the problem. I was part of the bureaucracy now. I was a state professor trying my best, getting tenure, but not offering meaningful changes. I was really involved in incrementalisms, tiny changes in the system, and I wasn't satisfied with that. Something was brewing within me. I decided that I would write for people who were going to make a change. I recognized that change would come through the investment community and through the free market. I saw that in this nation, where everything is basically subject to performance-based accountability, education wasn't. So, with an investment of $6,000, I published the first issue of *The Education Investor* in the summer of 1993."

In 1995, McLaughlin met Michael Sandler, an investor who was impressed with the publication. Sandler bought stock in the parent organization EIG, The Education Industry Group, LLC, after which the name of the publication was changed to *The Education Industry Report*. The infusion of that money made it possible for McLaughlin to leave his university position. Within eighteen months he was able to buy out Sandler; invite a young man, Mason Sorensen, to join the staff as part owner; add a consulting and research component; and grow the business to its present-day status as a leader in the worldwide, several-trillion-dollar education industry. McLaughlin also moved his company to free-market-oriented Sioux Falls, South Dakota, his wife's home area.

## Opportunity, Independence, and Integrity

Even today McLaughlin sees himself more as a teacher than a consultant. He likes to tell the story of how he once started a meeting of some ninety investors with a "teacher-like" question, one designed to get the attention of his "students": "What do unsatisfied consumers, poor performance on standardized tests, and lack of accountability produce?" His answer was, "Opportunity." McLaughlin feels strongly that the time is ripe for change. He believes that the emphasis is rapidly moving from schooling to learning, that no longer will education be measured in terms of days, hours, and minutes spent in classrooms, but in terms of demonstrated mastery of materials. He is convinced that the homeschooling movement is a significant breakthrough, as is the emergence of charter schools.

Currently, McLaughlin sees little difference between public schools and private schools. He remarks, "They don't look a lot different. Everything appears about the same. They're organized the same. The calendars are the same. The work is the same. They assess and evaluate progress the same way. In my opinion, the major difference is that private schools can be more selective. In the very near future, we will see some major transformations. We're going to see companies that will fill the gap between what is and what can be. We'll see virtual learning, online learning, creative learning centers designed to meet special interests and needs. There will be places and Web sites that make it possible for individuals to earn credit for all kinds of 'course work' on their own schedule regardless of day or hour. Tutors, currently a major portion of the for-profit sector, will be licensed to offer credit in their area of specialty. Parents, students, teachers, and lifelong learners will all be empowered to be increasingly in control of their learning."

Regarding future educational entrepreneurs, McLaughlin believes that there has never been a better time to envision innovations in learning or to establish new businesses in education. He offers the following insightful advice: "First of all, know your values are in the right place. Entrepreneurship is a roller-coaster. It's a ride. There are wonderful moments, and there are moments of significant worry and fear. Be prepared for both success and failure. Be willing to build upon both. Keep children at the center of your mission. If children are not at the center of your mission, then stay the hell out of the business. Remember, profit is OK, but money cannot be the only motivating force. People who put money above children are the robber barons of our profession. They are the enemies of children; they are the enemies of our industry. Integrity and quality are the only things that will help children and our industry. Integrity and quality will be the only things that will allow you to survive and grow as a force for good. If those values aren't in place for you, then don't even consider moving into the marketplace. And if you *are* thinking about such a move, now is the time to do it. Never has the opportunity been better."

In early 2000, McLaughlin sold The Education Industry Group, LLC, including *The Education Industry Report,* to edventures.com. McLaughlin felt that he had accomplished his mission. He had started the newsletter in 1993 in order to initiate dialogue between investors and the education marketplace. He had wanted to participate in shaping the emerging education industry and to help frame the discussion regarding education, children, society, and business. He is convinced that his vision and his publication have been invaluable to the industry.

Having founded a successful school in Nashville, served as a professor of education, and created one of the most vital publications in the education industry, McLaughlin has recently formed The John McLaughlin Company, LLC in Sioux Falls. Through this company, he advises investors and operating companies in the education industry. He continues to live by the motto he adopted years ago: "Help, enjoy, prosper."

# Chapter 16

## Shaping the Child Care Industry

### Green Acres

*Early childhood pioneer and child advocate*

**Dr. Grace L. Mitchell, Founder**

Few people have had the opportunity to help shape a new industry as Dr. Grace Mitchell has done for the child care industry. Mitchell, who has been a staunch advocate for quality child care in the United States, has been referred to as the "Grande Dame" of child care and affectionately called "Amazing Grace" by her friends.

Mitchell established one of the first nursery schools in the country and was a renowned educator and child development expert. In addition, she authored or coauthored eight books, six of which focus on early childhood education and child care, and with her son, F. Lee Bailey, Mitchell owned Telshare Publishing Company, Inc. Moreover, she has been a popular public speaker because of her ability to captivate audiences. The title of one of her books, *I AM! I Can!* reflects the essence of Mitchell's career and life.

#### Pioneering a Nursery School

After graduation in 1927 from the two-year Fitchburg Normal School, at age eighteen, Mitchell was faced with a tight job market. Consequently, she accepted a short-term substitute teaching position in a one-room school in Maine. There she lived and worked in primitive conditions on a farm with a family and had to walk two miles to school each day. According to Mitchell, "The only toilet facilities at school were twin outhouses — one for boys, one for girls — each of them two-holers. There was a well in the yard, and inside there was a sink with a hand pump in the corner of the classroom. The lids of the old wooden desks were scarred with initials carved by generations of local youngsters."

The following year, Mitchell landed her first regular teaching job in Brunswick, Maine, with a salary of $800 per year. Soon she discovered that new teachers were receiving $300 more per year in Massachusetts, so the next year she obtained a teaching position in Sharon, a bedroom community near Boston.

Ironically, Mitchell's concern for her students resulted in loss of her contract the following year. It was not renewed because she made it a practice to communicate with parents about the progress of their children, and in her school it was an unwritten rule that only the principal could communicate with parents. However, due to Mitchell's tenacity she was hired the next year by a neighboring school district as a substitute to teach second grade for seven dollars a day.

Knowing her substitute teaching job would be terminating at the end of the school year, Mitchell, who had an interest in children with special needs, took a course on the topic at Harvard. In this class she was influenced by the writings of Maria Montessori, who had designed educational programs for retarded ghetto children in Italy. Later, Mitchell used one of Montessori's concepts when she established her nursery school.

During the Great Depression in 1933, her husband's income was greatly reduced, which made it difficult for the couple to meet their financial obligations. Meanwhile, Mitchell was pregnant with her first child and unable to get a teaching job because school districts would not hire pregnant women.

It was at this time that one of Mitchell's sisters suggested that she start a nursery school. While considering this option, Mitchell read everything she could about nursery schools, finally deciding that opening a nursery school could supplement the household income as well as make it possible for her to both have a family and still pursue her career as an educator.

After her first child, Lee, was born, Mitchell decided to make one of the rooms in the five-room rental apartment into a nursery school. Next, after putting an advertisement for the school in the local paper but receiving a limited response, she obtained a list of members from her church and went door-to-door with her son, talking with parents about her "radical new idea" of opening a nursery school.

Soon Mitchell's nursery school opened with thirteen three-to-five-year-old children in addition to her son, who often amused himself on the floor while Mitchell provided activities for the other children. The nursery school's hours were from 9:00 to 11:30 A.M. and parents were charged one dollar a week for each child in attendance.

After a while, Mitchell's simultaneous roles as business owner, mother, and homemaker became too demanding, so she hired a helper referred to her by a friend, a person who had been afflicted with polio as a child and used crutches to get around.

After a year, Mitchell's business had outgrown the family's modest apartment, so they moved into an eight-room house. Despite the growth of her business, the Depression continued taking its toll to the point where Mitchell's husband lost his job and the family's only income was from the school. Finally, because the family could not pay their rent and bills, their gas, electric, and phone were shut off and Mitchell had to close her school. At the time, she was pregnant with her second child, Nancy. However, despite these setbacks and further additional responsibilities, Mitchell did not give up.

Soon a member of her church who was working for the Works Progress Administration offered Mitchell a job supervising children during the summer at one of the local playgrounds. Rather than just supervising the children, Mitchell began an arts and crafts program and conducted daily storytelling.

Then in 1936, the headmistress of a local private school for girls offered Mitchell free rent and a four-room apartment to operate a nursery school on the campus. Mitchell succeeded in achieving a full enrollment for the nursery school. However, when a new administration took over the school, she began looking for other locations for her school.

One morning Mitchell and her assistant took their eighteen nursery school children for a walk to a neighboring property. While there, they met the owner of the property. Mrs. Clark, a widow, took an interest in the children and invited Mitchell to bring them back frequently. After a few visits, Mitchell informed Mrs. Clark that she was looking for another location for her nursery school, and Mrs. Clark offered to let Mitchell use a building on her property. Mitchell decided an appropriate name for the school was Green Acres because of the lovely surroundings.

Needing capital, Mitchell approached a local bank for $250 to buy a secondhand station wagon for the school. The banker answered skeptically, "You mean mothers send their small children out of their homes and let someone else look after them?" However, after listening to Mitchell's plea, the banker prepared the check for the amount requested with the response, "I think I've just met the first woman business tycoon."

By 1941, the nursery school was financially sound, but that changed when Mitchell's third child, Bill, was born and World War II began. Because the country was now on rations, many daily necessities were difficult or impossible to buy, and Mitchell's attempt to both raise a family and be a business owner became more difficult. Moreover, around this time her husband's infidelities forced her to seek a divorce.

## Integrating Children with Disabilities

Despite the hardships, Mitchell assisted in the war effort. She received a call from the president of the Raytheon Corporation, a large electronics manufacturer, stating, "We must have women to maintain our machines if we are going to keep up with government orders. Someone has to take care of the children. I want you to take the children into your school." Mitchell's response was to change her half-day nursery school to a war nursery open from 6:30 A.M. to 6:30 P.M.

After the war, Green Acres continued to grow. In addition to the nursery school, Mitchell established a very popular summer day camp. Now she was operating a year-round program and needed to spend more time on programming, staff development, and other nonbusiness-related areas. So she hired Don Mitchell, a local teacher with a business background, as a part-time employee to supervise the bookkeeping for the school. Don had braces on his legs and walked using a cane because he had contracted polio as a child.

The working relationship between Grace and Don was respectful and harmonious from the beginning, and deepened as time went by. After a long courtship, they married. Grace exclaims, "With joy in my heart, I became Mrs. Donald Mitchell. My marriage to Don is one of the best things that ever happened to me."

During a community uproar that threatened closure of her school because of zoning problems, Mitchell changed the status of her privately owned business to a nonprofit organization. Commenting on the reason for the change, she says, "I had devoted fifteen years of my life to developing a school I knew was good for children, and I didn't want it to go out of existence if something happened to me."

Another one of Mitchell's remarkable accomplishments is that she was one of the first educators in the country to integrate children with disabilities, including the blind, into a school program. She reflects with pride, "We soon discovered that the few physically disadvantaged children were enriching the lives of their many so-called normal classmates."

### Innovating through Self-Assurance

By 1955, her school program had grown to the point where Green Acres had a fleet of fifteen station wagons transporting children to and from school. Both Green Acres nursery school and summer day camp were held in high regard. According to Mitchell, "We placed a higher value on imagination, spontaneity, and creativity than on rote learning. In day camp our goal was to create an oasis and a refuge where children could relax, have fun, and pursue their own interests, with more emphasis on utilizing the natural beauty of Green Acres than on competitive sports."

In 1970, Mitchell accepted an invitation to help organize and become cofounder and executive vice president of Living and Learning Centres, Inc., which eventually became a chain of forty-seven child care centers in New England. Mitchell's daughter, Nancy, who had two degrees in education, was also hired by Living and Learning Centres as the personnel director. Mitchell speaks with enthusiasm about that time: "Working in tandem with my daughter in the development of an exciting business proved to be one of the greatest joys of my life."

As vice president of Living and Learning Centres, Mitchell was able to implement her "I am! I can!" philosophy, which stresses the development of the individual. According to her, this philosophy "was encompassed in everything I thought, taught, preached, and followed in my daily life. It is because we are uniquely put together that we each have something to contribute. I believe there is a niche, a place in the sun for each of us. When the 'I am! I can!' is strong, that is when a person feels good about himself — his self-confidence allows him to venture forth, to take risks, and accept new challenges. Whether it is an infant taking his first steps, or a mountain climber who reaches the tallest peak, if he succeeds, his 'I am! I can!' expands."

Living and Learning Centres eventually sold to Kindercare, a large national child care company. Following the sale, Mitchell continued to be active by helping to establish the new Department of Early Childhood Education at Quinsigamond Community College.

In 1976, after agonizing over relinquishing control of Green Acres, Mitchell finally resigned her position as director. However, she continued to be involved with Green Acres as a consultant and member of the board of directors. At a testimonial party given in her honor, she said, "I'm resigning, not retiring. I believe that I still have some years left for growing, giving, and pleasuring." In 1986, Green Acres closed because its lease expired, and the Green Acres Foundation was established at Tufts University's Child Development Department. The stated purpose of the Green Acres Foundation is "To perpetuate the spirit and philosophy of Green Acres by assisting teachers of young children in their professional growth."

Mitchell is a convincing role model for lifelong learners. At age forty-five, when her daughter, Nancy, was graduating from high school, she received a bachelor's degree from Tufts University. At age sixty-three, she and her youngest son, Bill, received degrees from Harvard — hers a master's degree and his a bachelor's degree. They are thought to be the only mother and son to march in the graduation procession at the same time from Harvard. Moreover, three months before her seventieth birthday, Mitchell received a PhD in leadership and education from Ohio's Union Institute. During the time she was working on a doctorate, she visited 150 day care centers throughout the United States researching a project connected with her studies. The material she gathered formed the basis for her first book, *The Day Care Book: A Guide for Working Parents.*

In the 1980s while in her seventies, Mitchell was carrying three different business cards: one from Grolier Educational Services, where she served as an educational consultant traveling around the country giving speeches and conducting workshops in early childhood education; one from Child Care Management, Inc., which she and her daughter, Nancy, founded in 1981 to work with industries to set up child care programs for employees' children; and the third from Telshare Publishing Company, Inc., which she started with her son Lee, to publish her books on child care and early childhood education and his books on law.

In 1988, Mitchell's best friend, partner, and devoted husband passed away. Reflecting on what Don meant in her life, Grace says, "What I remembered most was Don's quiet composure and the firm grasp of his hand — it was the symbol of his love and support. When we were apart, or when I was struggling with a problem, thinking about the touch of his hand comforted me as if he had spoken. I realized that through his touch, Don had transmitted his strength to me, and I said a prayer thanking God for allowing me to share Don's life and love for forty years."

After her eightieth birthday, Mitchell's lust for life and her "I am! I can!" philosophy continued to prevail. She toured the United States with her sister, Lois Dewsnap, visiting child care centers to see what had changed since the 1970s, when she had evaluated child care centers throughout the nation in preparation for her doctorate. She also snorkeled in the Atlantic Ocean; camped on an American Indian reservation; took a raft trip down the Colorado River; parasailed in the Bahamas; flew in a hot air balloon in Sedona, Arizona; took ballroom dancing lessons; wrote three books; and was in the courtroom during the O.J. Simpson trial observing the legal maneuverings of her son F. Lee Bailey.

In 1999, at her home in Harbor's Edge in Delray Beach,

Florida, more than one hundred family members and friends helped Mitchell celebrate her ninetieth birthday, a party she fondly calls her "Birthday Bash." At the event Dr. Mitchell presented her autobiography, *Growing with Grace* to each person in attendance.

Throughout her career, Mitchell has been recognized for her contributions to education by numerous groups and organizations around the country, including receiving the prestigious "Living Legacy Award" in 1988 from the Women's International Center.

When asked what advice she had for educators considering becoming educational entrepreneurs, Mitchell stated emphatically, "Make certain that providing quality education for children is your primary motivation for going into business, and not just profit. Profit will come if you provide a quality product or service!"

Sadly, Dr. Grace L. Mitchell, a friend, renowned educator, and marvelous human being, passed away on January 27, 2000, at the age of ninety-one.

In informing friends of Dr. Mitchell's death, her sister, Lois Dewsnap, wrote, "Grace lived a wonderful life, with the knowledge that she was making life happier for thousands of children through the books she wrote, the speeches she made, and the example she set."

# Chapter 17

## Enriching Education for Special Needs Children

### Rossier School

*A school for children with special needs*

**Dr. Barbara J. and Dr. Roger W. Rossier, Founders**

Energy, experience, teamwork, drive, nerve, and creativity helped Barbara and Roger Rossier become successful entrepreneurs. What made them extraordinary was their vision of and passion for quality in education.

As schedules go, Barbara and Roger Rossier's looked busy and fulfilling in early 1980. Roger was working as a counselor at Cypress College in southern California; Barbara was teaching at the university level, expanding her private practice as a psychologist, and working in a public school as a psychologist. In addition, they were raising two children.

The average couple in such a situation would have warded off additional demands on their time and energy. But when the Rossiers were presented with an unexpected opportunity to go into business, they did not hesitate. "I happened to be talking to the director of special education for a school district in Orange County, California. He said, 'A local private special education school is for sale. Why don't you buy it?'" recalls Barbara.

Although the idea came out of left field, Barbara took it seriously. She says, "I thought, 'Hmm, that sounds pretty interesting.' Because I had supervised the nonpublic schools when I was working in the district, I knew that school, or thought I did. And it was a pretty good buy."

Ultimately, in 1980 the Rossiers purchased the small school, which served forty children with significant academic, social, and emotional delays. Over the years its enrollment grew to 200, and it became the focus of Rossier Educational Enterprises, Inc. By the time they sold the school in 1998, it was one of the largest therapeutic schools of its kind in the country and was noted for its high academic standards and top-flight vocational program.

This first step into entrepreneurship led to others. Over the years, the Rossiers also established a profitable real estate and leasing business, became involved in educational publishing, and operated an educational travel agency. In addition, to infuse what Barbara calls "balance" into their hectic lives, the Rossiers committed an impressive amount of time, energy, and financial resources to educational, civic, and philanthropic causes.

## Increasing Educational Options

The Rossiers' varied backgrounds in many ways prepared them to take risks and focus on innovative solutions to problems. Barbara Rossier was born in Casper, Wyoming. Because her father was in the construction business, the family moved often. As a result, she attended thirteen schools before she went to college, an experience that enhanced her natural ability to adapt quickly to new situations.

After working for four years in a law office with the intention of becoming an attorney, Barbara reconsidered her plans to maintain flexibility in her life. She recalls, "I thought, 'Is the world going to be a better place for my having been an attorney or will I leave it better if I'm an educator?' I obviously chose the latter." She proceeded to enroll at Brigham Young University to earn her bachelor's degree, which she did in two and a half years. As she explains matter-of-factly, "I needed to get through it."

Next, she obtained her teaching credential and taught in a junior high school in California. In 1960, she earned a master's degree in educational guidance from the University of Southern California (USC) while continuing to work as a teacher/counselor. In 1964, she became a counselor at Westminister High School in Orange County, California. There one of her fellow counselors turned out to be a young man named Roger Rossier.

"I liked her style," Roger says when recalling Barbara's directness, enthusiasm, and determination to make a difference. A California native and former GI, he had majored in education and physical education at California State University at Long Beach and then taught physical education and geography at various schools before earning his master's degree in educational guidance at USC. Ironically, Roger and Barbara had attended USC's School of Education at the same time but did not meet each other there.

The Rossiers married, and the couple continued to work at the secondary and college level while accumulating additional degrees from USC. In 1972, Roger earned his doctorate in higher education, having focused on vocational education. Barbara, who had earned a second master's degree, received her doctorate in 1971. She also earned additional teaching, counseling, and administrative credentials and obtained licenses as an educational and later a clinical psychologist. Teamwork has been a central part of Rober and Barbara's relationship — it enabled them to work, obtain advanced college degrees, start a business, and raise two sons.

In the late 1970s, Barbara opened a part-time private practice specializing in psychodiagnostic evaluation of children and adults with various developmental delays and disabilities. Soon two events would open the door to a future the Rossiers had not anticipated, but for which they were uniquely suited.

The first pivotal event was a change in leadership at the public school where Barbara was working as a school psychologist, one that left her feeling restricted professionally. Consequently, in August 1979, she resigned her position as school psychologist to expand her private clinical practice, while maintaining an assistant professorship.

The second catalytic event occurred when the school district's special education director suggested that Barbara purchase the nonpublic school that had just come on the market. Although neither Barbara nor Roger had any particular entrepreneurial aspirations, the idea intrigued them. Barbara's parents had been in the construction business, so the risks and benefits of business had been a part of her early life. Further, she had already demonstrated her organizational and fiscal savvy by setting up her successful private practice. Perhaps most importantly, the prospect of developing an educational program at their own school was irresistible to the Rossiers, who were determined to make a positive contribution to education.

"So we got it," Barbara says. "It was just that simple."

In order to maintain some consistency of income, they agreed that Roger would continue working as a counselor at Cypress College until his retirement at age fifty-five. Fortunately, some creative financing on the seller's part enabled the Rossiers to pay off their debt quickly. "The person who was selling the school had some economic needs and arranged interesting loans that turned out to be very beneficial to us. So we were able to purchase the school for what I think was a good price and we were able to pay it off rather quickly," Barbara explains.

## Meeting Students' Complex Needs

Subsequently, Rossier School was licensed to provide educational, counseling, and vocational services to children from kindergarten through twelfth grade whose needs could not be sufficiently met in neighborhood schools in Orange and Los Angeles Counties. However, the Rossiers soon realized the school's location behind a church in the city of Orange, California, was not suitable. So they initiated a search for a better one — a move that would involve the Rossiers in the real estate business.

"I immediately started looking for sites, and at that point school districts were closing schools due to declining enrollment," says Barbara. "We selected the ones we wanted and asked the district to put them up for disposal in the order we preferred, and the district granted our request. We were in the same site for eighteen years."

At this point, the Rossiers leased one property to their school. They also obtained three more sites that were being closed, leasing these and other properties acquired over the years. "Our tenants have been small schools, churches, and organizations that deal with public service. An infant center and preschool was opened in 1980 enrolling children between six months and six years of age. The infant program was one of the original infant programs in Orange County and grew to be one of the largest. A summer school was also added to the Rossier School's program. We don't do any retail or industrial leasing. The diversification worked well for us," says Barbara.

Meanwhile, the Rossiers focused most of their attention on the Rossier School. One issue they addressed almost immediately was a problematic two-tiered funding system they had inherited from the previous owner.

Twenty of the school's students were paying privately at a discounted rate, while the other twenty were publicly funded. The private pay rate was insufficient to cover the cost of services such as counseling, which the Rossiers considered essential and also put them in competition with the public schools, something they found undesirable. Consequently, they accepted only pupils referred by school districts.

The Rossiers emphasized a cooperative relationship with the public school system. "The only way I would enroll a student would be if a public school indicated that it did not have an appropriate school program and the child had an IEP (Individual Education Plan)," Barbara explains. "We would not enroll a child who was referred by a parent or an advocacy group. That was one of the things that helped us grow. The school districts had confidence in our integrity. Districts also valued the fact that one of our goals was to return the children to public school."

Although the Rossiers, astute financial decisions resulted in a more efficient business, running the Rossier School was nevertheless very demanding since it was in session all but seven weeks a year. They quickly mastered how to manage the many policy and administrative details of a growing business, and at the same time be leaders in the field of special education. The school had its own transportation system. All students in Orange and Los Angeles Counties received home-to-school transportation on a Rossier School Bus. Eventually they were running twenty bus routes within a radius of fifty miles. As licensed bus drivers, both Barbara and Roger took stints driving in the beginning, and Roger was certified to train the other school bus drivers. The Rossiers also supervised the school's food service, which met federal, state, and school district nutritional standards.

Even though operating the school presented many challenges, the Rossiers never regretted their decision to purchase it. "I know I'm a more well-rounded person. I think I'm healthier mentally and physically. I often say I don't think I'd be alive if I'd stayed in public schools, because it was so constricting," Barbara remarks.

Among other positive results, the school gave the Rossiers an opportunity to test and prove their own educational, management, and leadership theories. "Our school ran on participatory management. My job was to facilitate others doing the best they could do. If that meant personally going to get something a teacher needed, I would do it," Barbara reminisces.

The establishment and implementation of a comprehensive program for the students perhaps best reflected their managerial and leadership skills. Barbara explains, "Our niche was working with youngsters who had learning disabilities and who also, in some combination, might have had delays in social and emotional development. They can be very, very challenging. We worked to return children to public schools when they were ready and have them be successful. We were able to establish creative programs based on the philosophy and approach we used."

The Rossiers' approach stressed a combination of academic, behavioral, and counseling therapy. Academic therapy involved following the regular public school curriculum, setting high academic standards that were individually designed for each student, and providing a comprehensive vocational education program. Counseling sessions and behavioral therapy were integrated into the students' daily program by a staff of onsite therapists. Parents received daily reports about their children's successes and difficulties, with bus drivers contributing to the reports.

## Success through Clarity of Vision

As the school's reputation grew, so did its student body. Eventually it was serving 200 students. Despite its obvious success, the ebbs and flows of the special education system presented unique challenges in terms of staffing and cash flow. Barbara notes, "The growth was consistently upward, although there would be a year or two of slower growth that often followed changes in the funding model. Then after we had a slow period, it would always catch up, and we would be inundated. Enrollment would end up high in the spring and drop down in the fall, because we had graduated children and returned them to the public schools. There was definitely a pattern to it."

To meet their students' complex needs, the Rossiers maintained a staff of 115 to 125 employees. A credentialed special education teacher supervised instruction in each classroom, aided by two assistants. "We would not employ anyone without at least a BA degree to work as an assistant, whereas many similar schools utilized college students or bus drivers to work in the middle of the day," Barbara says, noting that most new employees had some training in human service.

The hiring policy helped attract qualified personnel, as well as encourage employees to further their own education. Barbara explains, "A significant number of assistants returned to college and obtained their special education credential while working with us. Some of them became our best teachers, because they knew the population."

In addition to hiring and motivating an excellent staff, Barbara identifies several keys to business success: "Have a very clear vision of what you want to do. Be service oriented. Think creatively and do everything at a very high quality. Maintain good public relations. And strike a balance between caring and profit. You don't do anybody a favor if you don't watch the bottom line."

In 1998, the Rossiers sold their school to Aspen Youth Services, although Barbara remains involved with the school as a consultant. They also continue to manage Rossier Enterprises, Inc.'s real estate activities.

Scaling down their commitments gave the Rossiers more time to indulge their love of travel, and they are now members of the select Century Club for travelers who have visited over 100 different countries. They raise orchids and are accomplished ballroom dancers.

In addition, their commitment to the University of Southern California has not wavered. A partial list of Barbara's volunteer positions includes being a member of the USC Board of

Trustees. She is also chair of the Board of Councilors for the University of Southern California Rossier School of Education, cochair of USC's California's Orange County Advisory Council, and past member of the USC Associates Board of Directors and the USC Alumni Association Board of Governors. Roger has been active in USC's Scion Scholarship Committee, supported the School of Education's recruitment efforts, and served as a mentor to graduates going into counseling. He is a member of the Athletic Board of Councilors.

The Rossiers believe in philanthropy. They established an endowed scholarship fund at USC in 1991 in the School of Education to assist master degree students training to become school counselors or school psychologists, and they launched a matching grant challenge program in 1996. In 1998, they made a $20 million gift to USC, which resulted in naming its school of education the Barbara J. and Roger W. Rossier School of Education. Their $20 million gift was the largest ever made to a school of education in an American college or university.

The Rossiers' style, whether they are volunteering or operating a business, has remained consistent: they become totally involved and demonstrate great generosity. Barbara responds, "We feel fortunate to have the financial resources to support various philanthropies, with our main focus being on USC." And just as they did in business, the Rossiers continue to assist USC in less prestigious projects. Barbara explains, "We're there to relieve the full-time staff and faculty. It's like doing the dishes and letting someone else do the cooking."

# Chapter 18

## Expanding Sports Education

### Future Stars, Inc.

*Making camping fun*

**Cathy Rush, Founder**

When Cathy Rush started a summer basketball camp for forty-two girls in 1971, she considered the venture a sideline. In 1977, by then a college coaching phenomenon, Rush took what she thought was a temporary break and ended up becoming an entrepreneur. Today, the business she established, Future Stars, Inc., is one of the largest sports camps in the nation, attracting more than 10,000 campers between the ages of three and eighteen to a variety of programs in Pennsylvania and New Jersey that offer sports and fitness, arts and crafts, academic enrichment, and just plain fun. The qualities that enabled Rush to achieve an outstanding record in her seven years as a college coach keep this educator scouting for the next entrepreneurial and educational challenge.

#### Camping with a Purpose

Rush grew up in New Jersey, received a BS in physical education in 1968, and an MA in education in 1972 from West Chester University in Pennsylvania. She began her teaching career at the high school and junior high school levels. When asked about what motivated her then and later, she says, "I always wanted to be a physical education teacher. I love sports, and I love teaching. Now I am a teacher running a camp, not a businessperson."

In 1971, she got the chance to indulge both of her passions, teaching and coaching, when she was hired to coach the basketball team at tiny Immaculata College, an all-girls' school with fewer than 500 students in Malvern, Pennsylvania, near Philadelphia. This was in the days when women's athletics received no coverage in the world of sports, a situation Rush helped to change.

Rush's subsequent achievements are impressive. Under her guidance, Immaculata's small but skillful teams made five trips to the AIAW Championship in six years, winning three national titles in 1972, 1973, and 1974. Overall, Rush had a record of 149 wins and 15 losses at Immaculata, where her players humorously called her "Amelia Earhart," because she frequently drove her personal station wagon that was used to transport her team past the entrances to where their games were being held and had to make U-turns to get to where the team was going to play. Five of her players during her tenure at Immaculata are now head basketball coaches in major college programs.

In 1975, she went on to coach the US Women's Basketball Team to a gold medal at the Pan American Games. In addition, Rush has earned numerous awards, including becoming one of the few women inductees in the Pennsylvania Hall of Fame and the prestigious Philadelphia Big Five Hall of Fame. She was also the recipient of a Special Achievement Award from both the New Jersey and Philadelphia Sports Writers Association as well as the Distinguished Alumnus Award from West Chester University.

Ironically, national legislation designed to give women more opportunities in athletics led to Rush's decision to leave coaching. In 1975, Title IX was passed, requiring colleges that offered men's scholarships to give women an equal number of scholarships. Immaculata was negatively affected by this change. Rush recalls, "In the early 1970s, no team that offered scholarships was allowed to play for the national championship. But in 1975, all the big universities — Penn State, Maryland, Villanova, and others — started offering scholarships, and the rules were changed to let them go to the national tournament. I went to the administration at Immaculata and said, 'We're going to need scholarships to continue the program at this level.' They said, 'You know, we don't think so.'"

The frustrated coach foresaw the demise of the program she had built at Immaculata. By 1977, her two sons were starting school, and she decided to take a break. She downshifted from the intensive demands of college coaching to a more relaxed schedule of running the summer basketball camp for girls she had started in 1971.

Camp enrollment had grown from 42 campers to 1,200 by 1977, largely due to the popularity of Immaculata's teams. In the beginning, Rush viewed this endeavor as a labor of love rather than as a money-making business, as a way of giving girls a taste of top-level coaching and competition. However, later she began to reassess the possibility of making it a profitable business.

### Combining Fun with Fundamentals

Rush's decision to become an entrepreneur in the camp business was the result of various changes in her personal life. "All of a sudden I had flexibility in my own schedule. I had afternoons, evenings, weekends," Rush recalls. "I said to myself, 'OK, I'm going to do this for one more year and then I'm going back to coaching.'" After that, she got divorced and felt her children needed her even more. At the time, there were perhaps a handful of camps in the country. But as enrollments continued to grow, Rush began to envision the camps as something that could help support her and her children and still enable her to be a full-time parent.

No effective coach sees an opportunity without seizing it, and Rush used every available resource to take advantage of this one. She knew she had the skills to organize a quality curriculum and hire good employees. She had already incorporated the sole proprietorship as a Subchapter S Corporation and named her company Future Stars, but to expand she needed financing.

"Initially, it was all out of pocket," says Rush. "When we needed brochures, I wrote a personal check or used a credit card. Soon this wasn't enough, so I went to a couple of banks and tried to sell them on the idea that I was going to be a good person to lend to. I ended up taking a second mortgage on my house, and that was my major source of funding."

Rush had been running her one-week residential camps in the Pocono Mountains of Pennsylvania, an area of wooded mountains long popular with tourists and campers. The leased facilities were rustic yet functional. She recalls, "The campers lived in cabins with showers down the road. There was a rickety old lodge with seven asphalt outdoor basketball courts and a little hut with one indoor court. If it rained, we bused kids to local high schools. It was just a funny time."

Rush's adaptability was very helpful in the late 1970s during the gas crisis. At the time, people could buy gas only on alternate days, and stations were closed on Sundays, which was the day the weekly camps began. Although this could have resulted in disaster for Future Stars, Rush salvaged the year's revenues by quickly shifting her campsite from the Poconos to Valley Forge Military Academy, which was about fifty miles closer to Philadelphia where the majority of the campers lived.

In the early 1990s, when the sports market was evolving, Rush again proved her ability to be visionary and to keep pace with change. With AAU tournaments becoming more prominent, youngsters no longer wanted to go to camp for two or three weeks, but for shorter periods that would allow them to attend tournaments. And since couples were having fewer children and more mothers were working full-time, Rush sensed that parents might prefer the greater flexibility and closer contact with their children that a day camp offered.

Serendipitously, about this time a representative of Immaculata College called to ask Rush if she would be interested in starting a day camp on campus, which had superior facilities. Rush quickly took advantage of this offer, and over time established camps on other campuses as well. Today, most of the Future Stars camps are nonresidential, operating on ten sites located on the campuses of colleges and other schools throughout Pennsylvania and New Jersey.

Rush's experiences as a teacher, parent, working mother, and coach have helped her expand her business in many other ways. First, she increased her potential market by focusing on more than sports. Future Stars now offers a variety of curricula serving children of many ages with widely ranging interests. Three year olds can stretch their muscles by participating in a variety of activities including swimming, and can use their creativity in group skits, computer games, arts and crafts, and treasure hunts. Older children can opt to work on science, computer, or fine arts projects and compete in intramural sports.

Despite the broader curriculum, sports remain a key element of Rush's enterprise. Future Stars Sports Camps offer an action-packed program that changes weekly. And the specialty sports camps for which the company is renowned feature personalized instruction to young athletes interested in honing their skills in the fundamentals and fine points of basketball, baseball, soccer, field hockey, tennis, and a variety of other sports. There are even basketball camps for entire teams, as well as invitational programs for elite athletes.

Another of Rush's marketing strategies was to build great flexibility into her scheduling and payment structure. Parents have a choice of which weeks or days of the week their children attend. "It's a scheduling nightmare, but that's our niche," Rush says. "People know that we can adjust to their schedules as opposed to them adjusting to ours." And even though it makes cash flow less predictable, Future Stars offers a sliding scale of fees, with the lowest paid well in advance and the highest reserved for last-minute decision makers.

In this cyclical kind of business, the marketing expenses are accrued in the first quarter of the year. For example, in January 1999 the company mailed out 150,000 brochures; went to camp fairs at schools; and advertised on radio, on television, in publications, as well as on billboards and the Internet. By contrast, most of the revenue is received in a few summer months.

In addition to developing effective marketing strategies, Rush and the staff must do an immense amount of preparation before the summer season. Given the shifting number and needs of campers, camp preparation takes much longer now than when Future Stars was first established. "The logistics are horrendous," Rush admits. "We have to order all the supplies for the arts and crafts, for the science experiments, and make sure we have the sports equipment we need. Then there are the camper T-shirts, counselor T-shirts — there's a lot of planning that takes place."

In this complex business, Rush's organizational skills, risk and frustration tolerance, and ability to attract and retain committed personnel have made the difference between success and failure. She credits her staff with making work a pleasure. Four full-time employees help with marketing and sales, data management, hiring and human resource activities, and curriculum and programming development. During camp season, Rush oversees 400 coaches, counselors, and other personnel.

## Instilling Aspirations

Future Stars continues to grow — in keeping with Rush's game plan. In 1998, the company experienced a nearly 50 percent increase in enrollment, which was almost enough to satisfy this highly competitive former coach. "It was the combination of a couple of good sites, some really strong marketing, and some great camp programs," Rush says. "Plus now we're getting kids who have been at our camps since they were four or five years old. They keep coming back, and a lot of them have siblings and friends that come along."

Such growth has made Future Stars a lucrative venture. But the enterprise has enriched Rush's life in other ways, too. She observes, "I get to have all these kids come every summer, and we think we do a great job in teaching them and giving them skills to go back and practice. During an all-star basketball camp in July 1998, we had a camp reunion, and there were seventy-five college coaches who had been Future Stars campers or staffers at one time. I look at what I've done and feel that I've touched more people than I possibly could have in a strict education environment. And for me, that's exceptionally rewarding."

In addition to running her business, Rush manages to give back to society through community service. A breast cancer survivor, she finds time to do public speaking and fund-raising for the American Cancer Society. Moreover, she is active in her local Rotary Club and donates to her alma mater, West Chester University, a portion of the revenue she raises from conducting a camp on the campus. She is frequently asked by local TV stations to be an announcer for college basketball games in the Philadelphia area and by national TV networks for NCAA basketball games.

Although Rush enjoys going to Florida to play golf during the winter when her business is less demanding, she never completely stops planning new strategies. "In the future we want to increase the number of sites and get more kids at each one. One possibility is to develop franchises," Rush hypothesizes, noting that each camp's program is prepared in meticulous detail between September and January. "We think we can sell the program to someone in a school or a school district that doesn't have the time or resources to prepare ten weeks of eight different events every day."

For would-be entrepreneurs, Rush's advice is straightforward and stresses the fundamentals. She states, "Know your market, the kinds of people you are going after. Be willing to spend a gazillion dollars and have confidence that you're going to get a return. Being an entrepreneur takes a combination of self-confidence and a willingness to risk it all. When you work for yourself, you work more hours. I would advise newcomers to surround themselves with people they like, which is why I look forward to going to work."

Reflecting on her decision years ago to sell a sporting goods store that was not meeting her expectations, she adds a final exhortation to future entrepreneurs — one that could have been delivered at court side after a bungled play: "When you don't do as well as you think you should, don't say, 'It was this or that.' Say, 'I messed up, and I'm going to do better.'"

# Chapter 19

## Pioneering Educational Publishing

### Frank Schaffer Publications, Inc.

*Developing quality learning materials*

**Frank Schaffer, Founder**

In 1973, Frank Schaffer needed to get a second job to supplement his elementary school teaching salary. He took a part-time instructor's position at Pepperdine University in southern California, a job that planted the seed for Frank Schaffer Publications, Inc. In 1994, he sold Frank Schaffer Publications, Inc. to a Canadian company for $56 million!

At the time of the sale, Schaffer's company was one of the largest and fastest-growing firms in the educational publishing industry, employing nearly 100 people and producing a wide variety of reading and other learning materials — a total of 950 products, 250 of which were nonbook products such as flash-cards, games, and puzzles.

#### Creating Innovative Student Aids

Schaffer grew up in New York City. After high school, he was inducted into the military and sent to Europe during World War II. At the end of the war, he returned to New York and married his high school sweetheart, Marilyn. Uncertain about what he wanted to do, for a time he sold phonograph records because he enjoyed music. Then one day a friend told Schaffer he was going to enroll at New York University to become a teacher. Schaffer decided to join his friend at NYU and got a BS degree in educational psychology, specializing in children with learning disabilities.

Soon Schaffer was recruited by San Diego County Schools in California as a special education teacher. Marilyn was pregnant at the time with their first child. The couple ended up living in austere conditions on an avocado ranch in San Diego County. The property lacked many conveniences, and the Schaffers even had to bury their own garbage. At school, Schaffer had fifteen students, many from an American Indian reservation. According to Schaffer, "They were supposed to be retarded, but they were no more retarded than I was. They just didn't score well on intelligence tests."

Later Schaffer was employed with the Palos Verdes Unified School District near Los Angeles, where he was a reading specialist working with first, second, and third grade students. There he kept other teachers abreast of new developments in the field of reading and gave them materials and strategies they could use with children who needed additional assistance.

To supplement his income, Schaffer began working part-time at Pepperdine University, where he taught graduate courses for teachers on the fundamentals of working with children who needed extra help in reading. According to Schaffer, "The teachers would come to my class very tired after teaching school all day, and I would write the course material on the chalkboard so they could accumulate as much information as possible. During one class in 1972, a student suggested, 'Why don't you put it down in a book? That would make it easier for us, and we wouldn't have to copy all your writing off the chalkboard. We don't understand your hieroglyphics anyway. And you're a New Yorker — you talk too fast for us.'"

## Making Learning Exciting

Subsequently, Schaffer decided to act on the suggestion and began developing worksheets that could be given to students, even having an artist put cartoons on them to add interest. During the summer of 1972, he used a typewriter with large print to put together a ninety-six-page book of reading activities. He found someone to do artwork and had 1,000 copies printed.

Soon Schaffer realized that with only twenty graduate students in his Pepperdine University classes, it would take forever to sell the 1,000 copies. He tried marketing the book to school supply stores, but they were not interested because he allowed teachers to reproduce and reuse his materials.

Then Schaffer found out about a learning disability conference held in Los Angeles in January 1973. Because he was not free to attend due to his work, Schaffer sent Marilyn to the conference to sell books. Soon she called Schaffer and informed him, "You are not going to believe this, but in the first hour and a half I sold three hundred fifty copies at five dollars apiece." Suddenly Schaffer realized that his venture could become profitable, and since outfitting five boys with tennis shoes on a teacher's salary was almost impossible, Schaffer thought, "If they really like my book, I can do more." This experience marked the beginning of Frank Schaffer Publications, Inc.

Once Frank Schaffer Publications, Inc. was established, it started doing direct mail. Labels were typed from school addresses obtained from the California State Department of Education, and orders started coming in slowly. Classroom learning centers, which help teachers individualize their instruction, were very popular, and teachers were looking for materials that could be incorporated. Schaffer's company was among the first to come out with activity cards that teachers could use with individual students. Within a couple of months these activity cards were a hot item, and orders came in rapidly from throughout the state.

During the summer of 1973, Schaffer employed teachers with good writing skills to produce materials for him. By October there were a dozen books available for teachers. According to Schaffer, "We were beginning to realize that this was really a company, and that it was going to provide us with a fairly nice supplemental income."

After the company took out a quarter-page advertisement in *Instructor*, a national magazine popular with elementary teachers, the business grew dramatically. "I got ten thousand responses from the ad from throughout the United States. We were in the direct-mail business big-time! People wanted our catalog, and I got a lot of orders," Schaffer enthusiastically recalls. At the same time, teachers were requesting Schaffer's materials in teacher supply stores, which opened up a new market for his products.

Schaffer worked long hours. During this time, on a typical day Schaffer taught until 3:30 P.M., tutored until 6:00 P.M., ate supper, wrote a couple of pages for future publications, and then packaged shipments until late at night. It was not unusual for him to have trouble finding the front door in the morning because of the mounds of packages to be picked up by UPS.

Originally the company was to be called Educative Materials for Fun, but since teachers were writing to Frank Schaffer at his home, and began associating the products with his name, Schaffer decided to use his name for the company. According to him, "It was probably just about the best thing we ever did, because we had a unique identity. Teachers can relate to a person, and teachers trust other teachers. When teachers find out that the president of a company has been a teacher, it always makes a big difference."

In the following years, Schaffer continued to build the company while teaching full-time. He attended educational conferences and conventions on the weekends in surrounding counties, where he displayed and sold his products. In addition, he sold his products from his home to teacher supply stores and by direct mail to teachers.

## Expanding the Range of Clients

In January 1975, after teaching for twenty-four years, Schaffer decided to take a leave of absence from the Palos Verdes School District so he could assess, with minimum risk, what the business could really do.

First, Schaffer moved the company out of the house and into an 800-square-foot building in neighboring Torrance, California. The following year, due to the dramatic growth of the business, the company was moved to a space of 6,000 square feet. As the business continued to grow, a large number of new materials were added to the product line. Authors hired to write new materials were paid on a royalty basis.

About this time, Schaffer realized that for the company to expand effectively he needed to focus more on finances. Consequently, the husband of a teacher in Palos Verdes, who had served as a business consultant to the company from the outset, was employed full-time as vice president of finance, freeing

Schaffer to concentrate on product development and marketing. Next, a graphic arts department was added, a computer was purchased, and a typesetter was employed. Finally, new product lines were developed such as math and phonics learning games, cross-curricular Literature Notes, and large floor puzzles. Schaffer reflects with pride, "The company grew each year, and we never had a bad year. With respect to growth, we did something very few companies do — personal performances. We never had any sales representatives. The vice president and I would fly into a city and negotiate deals with teacher supply stores on the spot. We always used a personal approach in representing our business."

Schaffer feels Frank Schaffer Publications is a recognizable brand like Nike sports shoes. Certainly its products are very distinctive because of the logo — a caricature resembling Frank Schaffer. It originated when one of his writers used a cartoon character for a product being made for the 1976 Bicentennial. Schaffer felt that the company needed a logo, and when he spotted a cartoon of a little man with a mustache, he decided to adopt it as the logo. Eventually he even grew a mustache to match!

Over the years, the business changed its approach from focusing only on teachers and elementary-age students to including preschool programs and parents, as well. According to Schaffer, "It's not just educational materials for teachers anymore: it is for parents, grandparents, nursery schools, and others. There has been a revolution of sorts."

During this time the company also changed its policy. When Schaffer first began the business, almost all of the sales were made at retail prices. But as the company continued to grow, most of the products were sold at wholesale rates. "I'd rather sell fifty books all at once at a discount to a school supply store than sell fifty books one at a time at full price," Schaffer states.

Originally catalog sales to teachers represented 50 percent of the company's business because school supply stores were not stocking Schaffer's products. However, as stores began to carry the extensive product line, direct mail became less important, and by the time the company was sold, sales directly to customers from the publisher accounted for only about 5 percent of total sales.

By 1995, when the company was sold to Harlequinn, a division of Torstar, Frank Schaffer Publications, Inc. employed more than 100 people. Schaffer was paid $56 million for the company, which was then doing $22 million in sales. Schaffer says he had always had a selling price in mind but did not think anybody would pay that much. A frugal person, he jokes that he really needed a lot of money to live on. Ultimately a buyer came around.

Recently, the Schaffers celebrated their fiftieth wedding anniversary and are rewarding themselves for their hard work by traveling extensively throughout the world. While they continue to reside in Palos Verdes Estates, California, their five sons, two of whom were active in the business at one time or another, live in Japan, England, Maryland, and southern California.

Schaffer's advice to educators considering becoming educational entrepreneurs is to work hard, stay competitive, and be tenacious — advice that reflects Schaffer's own successful approach to business.

# Chapter 20

## Offering Alternatives in Communication

### Warger, Eavy and Associates

*A multifaceted firm specializing in communication*

**Dr. Cynthia L. Warger, Founder**

In 1989, Cynthia Warger established Warger, Eavy and Associates (WEA), a full-service communications firm. WEA specializes in producing education-related products, which comprise about 90 percent of its work; the other 10 percent is reserved for small-business marketing and communications projects. For over ten years WEA has developed a variety of print materials, including books, training guides, reports, newsletters, press releases, catalogs, and sales materials. Many of the products are sold by commercial publishers. WEA also produces teleconference events and broadcast-quality videotapes for education, public relations, and documentary purposes.

From the small office in Reston, Virginia, comes a vast array of programs and products for a large number of consumers. The onsite equipment to support desktop publishing alone consists of state-of-the-art computers, printers, modems, and a high-resolution copier. An AVID video-editing studio and sound booth are located onsite for video projects. WEA is supported by long-time vendor relationships with other small businesses that provide secretarial services, printing, graphic art, copyediting, proofreading, packaging, and mailing. Local video production companies provide studios for taping, on-location videography, animation, sound mixing, and satellite broadcasting.

WEA has no-full time employees other than Warger, who purchases services from other entrepreneurs. When WEA accepts a project that requires a creative team, Warger creates a team of consultants specifically to meet the goals of that project. In this way she always has the best for the task.

The company's range of clients is impressive and as varied as the tasks performed. Over the years, WEA has worked with major education associations, government agencies, school districts, nonprofit organizations, commercial publishers, and private businesses. A sampling of WEA's recent contracts includes writing and producing the book *Early Warning, Timely Response: A Guide to Safe Schools,* which President Clinton mailed to every school in the country; producing a teleconference on educational technology between the US Department of Education and the Ministry of Japan; writing a guidebook for teachers pursuing National Board Certification for the NEA and AFT; producing a video documentary, *Promising Practices for Safe and Effective Schools,* which won the 1999 Communicator Award of Distinction; writing and producing numerous newsletters, among them *Claiming Children* for the Federation of Families for Children's Mental Health, *Research Connections in Special Education* for the Council for Exceptional Children, and *Afterschool Extensions* for the University of Miami. Along with all of this, Warger still tries to schedule her time and projects in such a way that she can also be available to design and conduct professional developments.

## Creative Avenues for Personal Expression through Art

How a business can successfully participate in such an assortment of projects and with so many clients is fascinating and enlightening. Certainly a major precipitant is Warger's wide range of experiences and interests. Warger's interest in education began when she taught drama, art, puppetry, and television to children and adolescents. "I developed and worked in many special programs, summer school programs, and community-based projects." Through this work she became aware of the power art has to provide avenues of personal expression for diverse groups of learners. She states, "I always worked with children who are diverse. Some came from the inner city; some were considered at risk; and many had disabilities. Art really allows children to celebrate who they are as individual spirits. It was great for the children and especially great for me. It confirmed my belief that all children are unique, they are all special. They are amazing."

She obtained a bachelor's degree from the University of Michigan with a teaching certificate in English and psychology. She earned her master's degree and another teaching certificate in special education from Eastern Michigan University. She did most of her public school teaching in the Michigan schools, where she worked at all school levels.

Warger's university work was as varied as her other experiences. While working on her doctorate at the University of Michigan, she continued her teaching in public schools and served as a teaching and research assistant at the university. There she directed a student-teacher training program, taught reading methods for children with reading disabilities, and coordinated one of the first university-level programs designed to reeducate professors in how to create and deliver instructional programs for students with disabilities.

In 1981, Warger was offered a position at the University of Toledo as a professor of special education. At Toledo she developed programs in behavior disorders and autism, as well as teaching a secondary education methods course. She also received one of the first federally funded grants to study collaboration between teachers.

In 1985, Warger applied to be editor of *Teaching Exceptional Children,* a prestigious professional journal for the Council for Exceptional Children. Assuming that editorship was something she would do as part of her university responsibilities, Warger was shocked to learn she would have to move if offered the job. "I called my husband. He was encouraging. He reminded me that because I had an MBA and master's degree in public policy, Washington, DC, would be a great place for me," she recalls. Warger eventually accepted the position, and in 1985 she and her husband moved to Reston, Virginia, where they live today.

Cynthia says with great pride, "The journal won two National Education Press awards for best journal special issue during that time. It was exciting to be part of that effort."

From there Warger took a position with the Association of Supervision and Curriculum Development (ASCD). At the same time, she continued her work as editor and consultant for the Council for Exceptional Students. At ASCD, Warger was on the executive staff for Program and Professional Development, where she oversaw all of the National Curriculum Study Institutes offerings, which were expanded during her tenure. She established the National Training Center and was responsible for its focus on early childhood. She also initiated the ASCD Satellite Training Events program and expanded the Human Resources Development Program. In her spare time she edited two books for ASCD.

### Adhering to Ethics in Business

In 1989, when her boss, Gordon Cawelti, announced his retirement, Warger left ASCD. Of that time she says, "Making the decision to become an entrepreneur using my own talents and my own resources was easy. Gordon was retiring. He was a great thinker — a futures thinker. I learned a lot from him. But I was ready for a change. While at ASCD, I had a lot of people asking me to work for them, which I couldn't do while working a sixty-hour week. So I decided that now was a good time to see if I could develop something on my own. That's what I did. During the first year, I actually earned a bit more than I had at ASCD. Since then, it has been extremely good, both financially and professionally."

Although after establishing WEA Warger was tempted a few times by job offers, she felt she would have had to give up too much to accept these positions. She recalls, "I just couldn't bring myself to give up my creativity and flexibility. When you work for an organization, it owns you. I still work for organizations; in fact, I like to work for organizations. When I work for an organization, I put 100 percent of my energy into it. I like completing a quality project and then turning it over to them. I might have my soul in it, but I don't own it. I think that is the educator in me; I know you can't own ideas. Once an idea is out there, it's the world's. As an educator, you want people to take an idea and make it their own."

Warger believes that having a strong vision and sound work principles are the most important factors for success. She takes pride in the fact that WEA has never agreed to any project that she felt might be damaging to children or educators. In fact, one criterion used when the company makes a decision to accept a project is whether or not that project respects educators, children, and their families. She reflects, "We have walked away from a couple of projects after they started. In some cases we lost some money but it was one of those ethical things. For me as a professional, I just had to do it." Warger considers her integrity tremendously important, convinced that without it she has little to offer her clients.

Warger is especially pleased with the relationships she has with many of the people who provide services to WEA. She says of these entrepreneurs, "It's been fun watching them grow. Some have provided services to me since 1985, even before I started my business. I think they feel the respect I have for them and what they bring to the table. All these people support me in doing what I do best: creating new programs, products, and publications."

Two important concepts that Warger has enlarged through the establishment of WEA are business and community. She says, "I used to think of myself as an educator and a consultant. Even though we serve clients nationwide, I now see myself as a person who also has a business in Northern Virginia. I am a viable part of the growth of the community, and I have grown with it. I have a different sense of belonging and commitment than I had previously. It feels good, and at least part of that feeling comes from being an active business entrepreneur. That is a dramatic change for me. It's a payoff I didn't expect."

## Maintaining Commitment to Community

Today Warger is grateful for her fulfilling professional life. Her work with schools, universities, and professional organizations has provided many opportunities for growth. In addition, she has been active in community efforts, including being the past president of the Reston Association Board (the equivalent of the traditional city council), participating in the Chamber of Commerce, cohosting a local TV program, and serving on the Fairfax County Community Services Board, which oversees and sets up policy and budgets for all mental health, developmental disabilities, and alcohol/substance abuse services in the county.

Asked about what advice she has for others interested in becoming an entrepreneur, she remarks: "A lot of people want change but they may not want to leave the safety of a full-time job. In that case they should explore alternatives. There are new opportunities coming from innovative school programs and local community projects. Many companies are supporting in-house training programs. Universities are interested in finding qualified mentors and practicum supervisors. Professional organizations are always on the lookout for people who have a variety of skills educators typically have. The first thing a person must do is ask, 'What do I want?' Then talk with people, network, ask questions. As opportunities arise, think about what is important and carefully consider the costs and benefits of any decision."

According to Warger, one of the stumbling blocks is finance. While noting that having sufficient finances is crucial, Warger also suggests that they should not always be the sole reason for making important decisions. "Over the years, I have watched business colleagues panic, immediately start searching for a traditional job, get one, and then express dissatisfaction because they missed having their own business. In many of these cases, they might have made some changes in their business — diversifying clients, reorganizing staffing patterns, investigating how technology might lead to reduced costs, and so forth — that would have gotten them through the financial crisis." She also stresses the importance of building a long-term business plan. "I have seen a number of entrepreneurs fail because they thought short-term. For example, they got a big contract, hired a lot of staff, and then couldn't sustain the company base once the contract was completed. They lost sight of being an entrepreneur and raced too quickly to being a business owner."

Further, Warger stresses the significance of having a network: "You need people to talk with. People you can trust. It is critical to have others with whom to discuss your ideas and concerns, your joys and sorrows. In a traditional job, people tend to think of their coworkers as extended family. When you are an entrepreneur, it's important to remember that clients aren't your network. They may become your friends, but they are still your clients. I have found that many of the vendors I use have become part of my extended family network. The volunteer work I do in the community also has helped me build the kind of network I find so important. You might become an entrepreneur, but that does not mean you do it alone."

# Chapter 21

## Accepting the Challenge of Disadvantaged Children

### Success Lab, Inc.

*Supplemental learning instruction for inner-city children*

**Kenneth E. White, Founder**

The death of Kenneth E. White's father, who retired at age sixty-five and died of a stroke four months later, was a turning point in White's transformation from a corporate climber to founder of Success Lab, Inc., which provides supplemental instruction to help inner-city children improve their academic performance. White says of this turning point, "It helped me recognize that I needed to do what I really wanted to do here, instead of moving along a path of riches and glory. It took me a while to figure that out. In the process, I owned a company and started my own consulting business in California. But I then realized that wasn't what I really wanted to do, either. It was just more of the same. My work wasn't leaving footprints."

As he searched for something to infuse his life with greater meaning, White began paying attention to some of the problems that most urban areas were having with education. He had gone to a high school on Chicago's west side, in an inner-city neighborhood where instead of a strong network of families, there were now drugs and gangs and despair — a fact that made the topic compelling.

Gradually he defined his mission to establish a for-profit company that would provide supplemental instruction to help inner-city kids improve their basic academic skills. He explains, "Historically, there is too much of an opportunity for less than desirable quality in a not-for-profit enterprise. We know that in any for-profit venture, if your product is not chosen by your customer, you go out of business. And one of the ways to assure that your product will be chosen is to have it be of high quality. So after very little thought, it was pretty obvious that in order to hold our feet to the fire in terms of showing customers we were committed to delivering a top-quality product that would meet their needs, we needed to do it in a for-profit manner."

Despite the challenges and trials over the past seven years, White's passion for his mission has not burned out. He states, "Several times a week, I drive through communities like the one I grew up in, and I am amazed at the number of school-age children and unemployed adults who are on the streets during the day. I often think, 'But for the grace of God go I.' There is so little separating the lives of these folks from my life. But the few differences add up to so much. These kids weren't given a choice of where they were born or are living. We've got to find a way to give them just as many choices as I had."

Since its establishment in 1993 to provide greater opportunities for inner-city children, Success Lab, Inc. has grown from a single facility to twenty-two school-based learning centers and seven other centers offering commercial-style supplemental instruction in the Chicago area. Success Lab's school-based students, who are at-risk or low-performing, have demonstrated an average reading improvement of nearly 1.4 grade equivalents after just forty-eight hours of instruction.

In the process of making the company successful, White has had to surmount numerous forms of resistance to innovations. He comments, "We've had a lot of traditional beliefs to overcome, and we've done a real good job of overcoming them. Sometimes you have to put your head down and just kind of run into the walls, and hopefully you can knock a few of them down. This is much easier if you have good results."

## Strengthening Inner-City Education

White attended the University of Iowa on a football scholarship. When he graduated in 1969, White became involved in the computer industry, which was gathering momentum at the time. He began his career as a programmer and progressed to a systems consultant before going to work for Blue Cross–Blue Shield, where he climbed his way up the corporate ladder.

After his father died and the direction of his career no longer seemed alluring, White embarked on several entrepreneurial ventures and did a lot of reading and thinking. Fascinated by the need to improve the educational opportunities available to urban kids and their families, he felt compelled to get involved. Consequently, he went to work for American Learning Corporation (ALC), an Encyclopedia Britannica company that operated Britannica Learning Centers throughout the United States.

White soon began overseeing Britannica Learning Centers in the Los Angeles area, then in 1990 moved on to manage the nine centers in Chicago. He says, "I actually learned everything I know about teaching through working with Britannica. I didn't have years of lectures on education theory. I was thrust into it. I can still recall the tremendous fear of sitting at a table with three kids staring you in the face wanting answers. What an awesome responsibility! How do you convey this concept? How do you help a child master a skill? It was amazing!"

White learned first by practical experience, then by studying theory. Along the way, he came to revere what he calls "real education and the folks who were committed to it." But as he talked to more educators and administrators and visited more schools, he grew increasingly distressed by the unmet needs of inner-city students. He recalls, "I saw a gap, a wide chasm, between what we knew and were doing in the learning centers and what was happening in the schools."

White believed that individualized supplemental instruction could transform the lives of at-risk and low-performing students. However, most inner-city students did not have such opportunities in schools, and economic barriers prevented franchisers from locating affordable commercial learning centers in their neighborhoods. "I saw a tremendous opportunity to help kids and to create a business," says White. Consequently, he decided to take his services into the schools, focusing on elementary school reading skills, because they formed the foundation for future academic achievement.

White settled on a name for his company years before he was in a position to establish it. He reminisces, "I was sitting at my desk at home envisioning what I wanted to accomplish with kids and how to do it. I wrote three or four columns of words and then began associating them. 'Success Lab' jumped out at me, and that's been the name since day one."

## Giving Students Credit for Success

Although White founded Success Lab, Inc. in 1993, he did not immediately try to sell its services to the schools. Instead, he opened one learning center in Park Ridge, Illinois, a suburb of Chicago, to use as a research lab. Between 1993 and 1995, his staff gave customized reading skills instruction to a wide variety of students including wards of the state of Illinois, low-income, middle-income, and even affluent families. Some had a solid skill base, while others had never owned a book or had anyone read to them. "We continually modified and fine-tuned our program looking for what worked consistently with all kids. What we discovered is that our method works and it works with students from any economic group, in any grade, and with any existing skill set," White reports.

In 1995, White began looking for a school that would pay him to operate a Success Lab Learning Center to improve students' reading skills. He began on the west side of Chicago, because he was familiar with it from his childhood. Dr. Sandra Givens, then principal of Spencer Math and Science Academy, was the first to contract with Success Lab. "Many principals didn't believe that a small company with one learning center and a president out selling every day could actually bring about changes that MacMillan or McGraw Hill couldn't. But Dr. Givens took a chance, and we were very successful there," recalls White.

Gradually, White also obtained contracts with other schools. His pitch focused on partnering with the schools to help kids break the cycle of failure, and Success Lab's performance proved that he could accomplish that. White notes, "The schools are responsible for teaching reading, writing, and arithmetic, but they are also expected to teach a great deal more— health, character education, physical education. The kids are performing poorly in reading, and yet there's a limited time each day for them to get instruction they need. Aware of all this, we told the schools, we're going to increase the basic reading skills of your kids so they'll perform better in school, in the classroom, and on achievement tests. We also told them that we're sure to make a difference since this is all we do."

One question many principals asked was what guarantee of improved test scores was Success Lab offering. "That was a big hurdle to overcome," says White, "because we weren't a test-prep company. I always said, 'What we're going to do is increase your kids' basic reading skills. Because of that, they're going to feel better about themselves, discipline issues are going to fade, and you're going to develop a well-rounded student. At the back end of all of this, achievement scores are going to increase.' And that's what has happened."

Success Lab's contracts have ranged from about $150,000 per year for 90 students to $175,000 per year for 120 students — a significant expense, especially since the money comes from the schools' discretionary funding. Still, the company has never been asked to leave a school because of unsatisfactory performance, or for any other reason. Currently, there are twenty-two Success Lab learning centers in schools, including five in private schools.

For their investment, schools get a self-contained turnkey program that provides students with an average of two hours of instruction per week in a three-to-one student-teacher ratio. Success Lab refurbishes the facilities to be used as learning centers, repainting walls, putting up colorful boards and posters, and supplying furniture, computers, and instructional materials. At each site there is a full-time program director and a staff of state-certified teachers trained in the Success Lab methodology. Success Lab also provides a Teacher Resource Center for the school's teachers. The program's director and instructors integrate themselves into the school culture by attending staff meetings, communicating regularly with classroom teachers and administrators regarding student performance, and participating in extracurricular activities.

In addition, Success Lab involves parents in all phases of

the program, so that they can contribute to and share in the students' progress. The program's director communicates with parents regularly through conferences and telephone conversations, and holds parent workshops on topics such as how best to help kids with homework.

From the students' perspective, Success Lab provides plenty of one-on-one attention and encouragement in a risk-free, comfortable environment. Before any instruction begins, a comprehensive diagnostic skills assessment is performed to identify a student's current reading skills. Success Lab staff also determine whether the student is an auditory, visual, or tactile learner. Next, an individual instruction plan is formulated and discussed with teachers and parents. Then progress is assessed after each hour of instruction, to prevent time from being wasted on unproductive activities or approaches. White says of Success Lab's strategy, "We start at a point where the student is being challenged just a bit. Then we ensure that during each hour of instruction every student is working on the precise content needed, at exactly the right level of difficulty, and in the proper learning style or modality to enable the greatest possible gain."

While making inroads at getting his reading instruction program into elementary schools, White was also running a full-service commercial program in Success Lab's original Park Ridge Learning Center, which was open on weekday evenings and Saturday, serving students from grades one through twelve. This program likewise used Success Lab's assessment and instructional methodology and provided instruction in reading, basic and advanced mathematics, study skills, writing, and ACT test preparation.

White believed that many inner-city parents would like to give their children the extra educational support that a Success Lab Learning Center provides if it were more affordable and more conveniently located. He calculated that he could offer the same high-quality services for as little as one-half the price and still remain profitable, as long as there was a way to reduce Success Lab's real estate occupancy and marketing costs.

With this in mind, White approached businesses where families and children tended to congregate, such as McDonald's, Burger King, Crown Books, and Barnes & Noble, and asked for free retail space, arguing that both parties would benefit. Although he did not find space this way, he was successful with the Chicago Park District, which told White, "We have space in hundreds of buildings throughout Chicago. Why don't you look around and see if you can find some communities where you would like to locate your centers."

As a result, in 1998, Success Lab signed an agreement to open five new commercial learning centers in park district facilities, all of which were located in inner-city areas never before served by such a program. Subsequently, one of the schools that had contracted with Success Lab took an innovative step by asking Success Lab to keep its learning center open after school and on Saturdays. Complying with this request, Success Lab was able to provide commercial learning center opportunities to another community.

Given its excellent track record, White foresees a positive future for the business. "We will certainly continue our growth in schools, both because of the quality of our program and because the political climate is becoming more receptive to private initiatives in public schools. We'll also expand our commercial operations, and we're investigating the possibility of going into other Midwestern cities, like Cleveland, Detroit, and Milwaukee," he explains.

Although White had important reasons for choosing a for-profit business model and his entrepreneurial skills have been important company assets, he prefers to emphasize qualitative factors when discussing the reasons for Success Lab's continuing growth. He says, "Number one, we give kids a lot of small, successful experiences in an academic setting. Number two, we give them a way to attribute those successful experiences to themselves as opposed to a teacher. That's radically different from what has been happening in the classroom. When you talk to parents, what you often hear is, 'My child didn't do well last year, but he's doing better this year because he has a good teacher.' We look at it from the kids' perspective and give them every opportunity to say, 'I do well because I'm good at reading! I do well because of *me.*' "

White offers two guiding principles for potential entrepreneurs. He states, "First, make sure you go into something you love, something that has meaning to you. If you do, your passion will help sustain your energy over the long haul. Toward that end, find and motivate good employees, and persevere when a solution isn't obvious. Second, make sure you deliver quality. Of course, it is essential to pay attention to other things, like pricing and appearance, but the only way to ensure that your product will be chosen by your customer is by striving for high quality."

# Chapter 22

## Promoting Private Practice for Educators

### Association of Educators in Private Practice

*A resource for educational entrepreneurs*

**Chris Yelich, Executive Director**

To the extent that today's aspiring educational entrepreneurs face fewer obstacles than their predecessors, they can be grateful to energetic and outspoken innovators like Chris Yelich, the executive director of the Association of Educators in Private Practice (AEPP). When Yelich helped found the organization in 1990, the concept was very new. She says, "When we told people our organization was about teachers going into business for themselves, they gave us the most amazed, quizzical looks, because nobody thought about that then." In the beginning, the association only had sixteen members — some not in private practice themselves, but dedicated to the organization's mission of advancing and promoting private practice teaching as an alternative career path.

Yet despite the difficulties of blazing new trails, the AEPP founders' passion for educational change was so keen that they perceived promise even in seemingly disappointing situations. For example, their first annual EDVentures Conference attracted fewer than twenty people, ten of whom were speakers. However, instead of lamenting the small turnout, everyone gathered around one big table in a conference room and brainstormed all day. "It was so motivating for me, because I could see that the idea did have potential," Yelich recalls.

Gradually, the organization grew and by 1999 had blossomed into a vibrant nationwide network offering its more than 600 members a three-day annual conference, as well as a wide range of networking and professional development services. Today, the majority of its members are in private practice in various settings from pre-K to adult education.

## Neutralizing Resistance to Innovation

Yelich's commitment to quality education began when she became a parent of two children. Then a medical technologist working in a hospital, she was appalled by the lack of emphasis on science in schools. She responded by volunteering in the classroom and monitoring the district's decisions, attending so many school board meetings that the members appointed her to fill a vacant seat, to which she later was elected. When she went back to school intending to switch careers to hospital finance, Yelich realized she was hooked on education. Consequently, she changed course and got her certification in secondary education as a science teacher.

After Yelich began teaching science in a Wisconsin private secondary school, she saw a need for more hands-on science at the elementary level. "Students didn't like science because they never had it," she states. Using equipment from her medical lab background, she began designing kits for younger children, calling this program Science Capsule. She was ready to "hang out a shingle" as a science teacher, when she made a disturbing discovery. Every other professional had options: you could go to work as an employee or you could start your own business and get the satisfaction of being accountable for your own services. However, in teaching, the only avenue open for someone who wants to teach was to work as a school employee for the rest of your life. "I wanted more control of my own destiny," Yelich says.

As a result of these insights, in 1987 Yelich attended a workshop with other like-minded educators, administrators, and school board members. Afterward, some met informally until June 1990, when they established the AEPP (originally called the American Association of Educators in Private Practice) as a not-for-profit corporation. To avoid the appearance of being a fly-by-night organization, the AEPP recruited some well-respected educators as associate members and contracted with an association management firm to handle administrative duties.

Although many Wisconsin lawmakers were more open than those in most states to the concept of educators in private practice, the AEPP's founders still faced resistance. For example, some of their friends who were school board members or educators in public schools expressed fears that the AEPP would steal the best teachers by promoting entrepreneurship. Yelich sought to ease these fears with facts that brought the matter into clearer perspective. She recalls, "I said I didn't think that by encouraging private practice you would take the best teachers. I thought you would attract teachers who were entrepreneurial. I told them only about 15 percent of people nationwide want to be in business for themselves; many people are satisfied working for someone else; and the same is true of teachers. But it is really important that we don't ignore that 15 percent of entrepreneurial-minded teachers, because they could be the ones to give education the jolt it needs, to provide a little competition and a little motivation for improving the system."

Yelich encountered additional opposition while testifying at the Wisconsin State Legislature and talking to groups about how private practitioners could serve remedial, specialty, and enrichment roles. She remarks, "There are people who just don't see how this could work. Some from the teachers' unions feel really threatened. Many times, administrators and people from higher education are so ingrained in the status quo and the way things have always been done that they can't even see another option. It is really frustrating."

Because resistance to the AEPP's concept from school districts made contracting with public schools difficult, the AEPP's focus shifted. The association's founders originally envisioned teachers contracting with school districts to teach science, math, English, and other specialties, but when that potential market seemed to be closed, the organization redirected its efforts toward the private and not-for-profit sectors. In this regard, the charter school movement helped. Yelich explains, "The charter school movement really helped us get our foot in the door, because charter schools, for the most part, can contract for educational services."

Learning to operate as an organization, the AEPP gradually gained momentum, attracting nearly ninety members by 1992. At this time, the association went through organizational and financial changes. When the services of the association manager proved too expensive, Yelich, who was still teaching and operating Science Capsule, moved the AEPP office into a spare bedroom in her home and handled most of the administrative duties, including the 800 number and the database. For years she and other board members, determined not to let the idea die for lack of adequate revenue, absorbed the organization's expenses.

In essence, the AEPP became another entrepreneurial venture, especially in 1994 when it began growing rapidly. Yelich recalls, "It was really stressful at times for my husband and children, but they were very supportive. We always try to give each other the freedom to pursue our dreams. And the reward? It's been fantastic working with such a great group of people."

A majority of today's more than 600 AEPP members have taken the plunge, either full-time or part-time, into for-profit or not-for-profit private practice. Some operate charter schools and tutoring centers, while others contract for such educational services as special education, math, science, and foreign languages, or for management and other administrative services. Additionally, the organization has a large number of members who simply want to support the AEPP's mission or may be contemplating going into private practice in the future.

## Expanding Opportunities for Innovative Educators

The annual EDVentures conference has expanded to a three-day event, to which people come for inspiration and networking with other educators, industry leaders, media personnel, and financial investors. Publications of the AEPP include its newsletter, *Enterprising Educators*, a detailed *Index of Opportunities*, and an association directory that gives members access to like-minded educators in their region or business sector.

Members also may advertise their practices on the AEPP Web site, take advantage of the association's group liability insurance, and call an 800 number to get information about their legal, marketing, insurance, or startup concerns.

During the next five years, the AEPP anticipates offering even more services to support educational entrepreneurs, including technical assistance in writing contracts. Yelich says, "We want to build our membership by reaching out to all those in educational private practice. Educational entrepreneurs often feel very alone. Belonging to an organization like this is a great way to share entrepreneurial spirit, swap ideas, learn the nitty-gritty of running an education business, and keep abreast of such breakthrough changes in our education system as charter schools, new school leadership, and the emergence of education as a Wall Street investment industry. Eventually, we would like to see our organization recognized by the public and accepted by the education community, so that our members can display the AEPP certificate and it would mean something."

"In recent years, many AEPP members have significantly expanded their businesses," Yelich adds proudly, noting that they have done it on their own merits instead of being tied to school employment. And while other members may not make as much money as they would have had they stayed in the school system, with its security, salary schedule, tenure, and benefits, Yelich has observed something important about both groups. "They are happy," she notes. "And happiness is a real and tangible thing for them."

According to Yelich, the time is right for teachers with an entrepreneurial bent to offer creative alternatives to the education system. She says, "The nation's economy is good, so people have more disposable income. And people are having children later in life when a lot of their own needs have been filled. They're willing to do what it takes to be sure their children receive a good education, because they realize how important that is for the future."

Yelich's description of a successful educational entrepreneur's attributes could just as well be applied to herself. "Enthusiasm and energy are what always come to mind, plus a belief that all children and adults can learn. If your prime motivation is money, you might as well get out, because that isn't going to work. You need passion to make it through the lean times," she remarks.

Yelich's passion for what she does is evident when asked why she speaks more about improving education or learning than about improving schools. "I don't believe all learning takes place in schools, or in the same way. We know how to teach all children, with all their different learning styles, but the schools are stuck. There is no incentive for schools to change because the kids cannot leave — the school holds them hostage, whether or not they improve. I think education is just going to leave that school behind. Kids are going to start learning on the Internet; they are going to start learning in many other places too. I don't know how long it is going to take, but I think it is inevitable," she says.

# Epilogue

## Entrepreneurship . . . and You

This book celebrates the lives of successful educators who, through creativity and hard work, have translated their visions about learning into viable businesses. Those businesses, and the processes the entrepreneurs used to establish them, serve as examples for others who may be reassessing their careers in education.

The educational entrepreneurs featured in this book differ considerably each from the other, yet also have much in common. All have made personal decisions to separate themselves from institutional education and become successful business owners. Yet their situations varied greatly in terms of their personal circumstances, the support systems available to them, as well as the products, programs, services, or technologies they developed.

However, they have numerous similarities. Each maintained the initial motivation for choosing education as a profession. The goal of helping children remained constant despite the differing strategies used to achieve this goal. Because they asked themselves what they could do to improve learning instead of what they could do to improve schools, their responses to possibilities were more uninhibited and unshackled. They were free to create, develop, and produce within the context of possibilities rather than impossibilities.

All the educational entrepreneurs profiled made sure they had a valuable idea or vision, one that could positively affect learning. And they all had to face the problems of finding the necessary financial resources to keep them afloat during periods when business was limited. Further, they had to find ways to publicize and market their efforts and decide whether to organize as a corporation, a partnership, or a sole proprietorship. Moreover, they had to resolve business problems concerning such details as payroll taxes, leases, personnel policies, equipment needs, and copyright issues. Finally, they had to learn how to make difficult choices, often based on limited data. This process forced them to increasingly trust their own ability to find solutions to problems.

These entrepreneurs as a group saw the value of seeking a balance between individual autonomy, networking, and social responsibility. They learned to take pride in their autonomy, discovering that the sense of personal control, responsibility, and growth that comes from being an entrepreneur made their sacrifices worthwhile. At the same time, they learned the importance of associating with and employing talented and creative people. Finally, following their personal successes, they all felt the need to give something back to their communities.

If the examples of successful entrepreneurs in these pages inspire other experienced or future teachers to take a fresh look at their chosen profession and their role within it to determine if their present situation is sufficiently satisfying, then this book will have served its purpose. Such an assessment must be careful, thoughtful, and honest, exploring an individual's values, beliefs, interests, energy, and level of commitment.

Educators who have the vision and drive to bring a new product, program, service, or technology to the marketplace should ask themselves if there is a need for it. To honestly answer that question they must be willing to do the necessary research to determine the potential of their idea. They should then test their idea with friends and others who have started a business and whose judgment they respect. After they are satisfied their idea has merit as well as business value, they should begin to develop a business plan.

Although some of the educational entrepreneurs featured in this book did not have a formal business plan when they first established their company, we highly recommend that any future entrepreneur develop such a plan as soon as possible. A well-developed business plan will put an entrepreneur ahead of the competition and serve as a communication tool for people interested in the venture. Moreover, formulating a business plan allows an entrepreneur to do the appropriate research and take a critical view of the proposed venture. Later the plan can be used as a "road map" in conducting the business and as convincing evidence of a worthy venture when approaching banks and potential investors.

A business plan addresses the key questions: where, why, how, when, who, and what. It is as important as the product, for it helps define what an entrepreneur wants to do. It forces the entrepreneur to:

- Translate ideas and thoughts into writing
- Take a critical look at the competition
- Research the industry
- Determine personnel requirements
- Research government regulations
- Determine who will be the company's attorney and accountant
- Develop the necessary marketing and sales plan
- Determine the corporate structure
- Complete monthly and annual pro forma income and cash flow projections

When we started researching this book, we contacted each of the profiled educational entrepreneurs with a set of written questions to ensure an effective interview. Because each participant subsequently said that the questions were extremely useful when reflecting on their activities as an entrepreneur, the questions have been adapted for inclusion here as a guide to other potential entrepreneurs. The questions are the same, only the tense of the verbs has been changed. Read them in good health, have fun dreaming, and seriously consider what they mean to you as you think of your future.

## Self-Interview Questions

- What is your educational background?
- What is your professional history?
- Describe the product and/or service you want to develop.
- What are the forces encouraging you to pursue your interest?
- Who is encouraging you?

- How much money will you need?
- What will be the source of that money?
- How do you plan to market and grow the business?
- How will your educational background help you in your entrepreneurial efforts?
- What problems, challenges, and rewards do you anticipate?
- What personal rewards will you forfeit when you become an entrepreneur?
- What new rewards do you hope to achieve?
- How do you see your product/service contributing to education and society?
- What other activities, besides teaching, have you tried?
- How will your personal life be affected?
- What is your business philosophy?
- Why do you think your company will be successful?
- What advice do you think you will need as you become an educational entrepreneur?

The future is yours. It is up to you to decide how you will make a difference. Regardless of that decision, we implore you to recognize that this kind of personal responsibility and the right to make your decision can happen only in a free society. It is through education that we can best protect that right.

# Suggested Reading

Anderson, Phillip H., David A. Beveridge, and Timothy W. Scott. *Threshold Entrepreneur: A New Business Venture Simulation.* Upper Saddle River, NJ: Prentice Hall, 2000.

Bhide, Amar V. *The Origin and Evolution of New Business.* New York: Oxford University Press, 2000.

Cook, Robert A. *Small Business Formation Handbook.* New York: John Wiley & Sons, 1999.

Coulson, Andrew J. *Market Education: The Unknown History.* New Brunswick, NJ: Transaction Publishers, 1999.

DeThomas, Art. *Financing Your Small Business: Techniques for Planning, Acquiring and Managing Debt.* Grants Pass, OR: The Oasis Press, 1992.

Drucker, Peter F. *Innovation and Entrepreneurship: Practices and Principles.* New York: Harper & Row, 1985.

Edmunds, Gladys. *There's No Business Like Your Own Business.* New York: Penguin, 2000.

The Entrepreneur Magazine. *Small Business Advisor,* 2nd ed. New York: John Wiley & Sons, 1995.

Fortgang, Laura Berman. *Take Yourself to the Top.* New York: Warner Books, 1998.

Gill, Michael, and Sheila Paterson. *Fired Up! The Proven Principles of Successful Entrepreneurs.* New York: Penguin Books, 1996.

Guzik, Ronald E. *The Inner Game of Entrepreneuring.* Huntington, WV: Upstart Publishing, 1999.

Harrell, Wilson. *For Entrepreneurs Only: Success Strategies for Anyone Starting or Growing a Business.* Hawthorne, NJ: Career Press, 1994.

Kishel, Gregory, and Patricia Gunter Kishel. *How to Start, Run and Stay in Business.* New York: John Wiley & Sons, 1998.

Krass, Peter. *The Book of Entrepreneurs' Wisdom: Classic Writings by Legendary Entrepreneurs.* New York: John Wiley & Sons, 1999.

Lonier, Terry. *Smart Strategies for Growing Your Business.* New York: John Wiley & Sons, 1999.

Price, Courtney, and Kathleen Allen. *Tips & Traps for Entrepreneurs.* New York: McGraw-Hill, 1998.

Salvaneschi, Luigi. *Location, Location, Location: How to Select the Best Site for Your Business.* Grants Pass, OR: The Oasis Press, 1996.

Sharma, Poonam. *The Harvard Entrepreneurs Club: Guide to Starting Your Own Business.* New York: John Wiley & Sons, 1999.

Stacey, R. *Managing the Unknowable.* San Francisco: Jossey-Bass, 1992.

Stolze, William J. *Start Up : An Entrepreneur's Guide to Launching and Managing a New Business,* 5th ed. Franklin Lakes, NJ: Career Press, 1999.

Zuelke, Dennis C. *Educational Private Practice: Your Opportunities in the Changing Education Market.* Lancaster, PA: Technomic Publishing Co., 1996.

# About the Authors

**Donald E. Leisey, EdD,** has been an educational entrepreneur for more than twenty years. He founded and served as chairman, CEO, and majority owner of Merryhill Schools, Inc., which was operating twenty-two schools when the company was sold to a publicly traded company in 1989. Leisey is currently the founder and owner of The Report Card, Inc., which operates educational resource stores in northern California plus catalog and Internet sales (www.reportcard.net). He has been a management consultant to many public and private schools. Dr. Leisey is an investor, serves on boards of directors of for-profit and nonprofit corporations, and is codirector of the International Academy for Educational Entrepreneurship.

Prior to becoming an educational entrepreneur, Leisey served for twenty years in various educational capacities in Pennsylvania, California, and Japan, primarily as a teacher, principal, assistant superintendent, business manager, and university instructor. From 1973 to 1979 he was superintendent of schools for San Rafael City Schools in Marin County, California.

Leisey received a bachelor's degree from West Chester University, a master's degree from Villanova University, and a doctorate in education and certificate in school business administration from the University of Southern California.

**Charles W. Lavaroni, MS,** has been active in education since 1949, when he first started teaching in California. In the ensuing years he has served as an elementary school principal, assistant superintendent, and superintendent in the public schools of California. He has also been director of teacher education and dean of admissions and financial aid at Dominican College in San Rafael, California. He received his BS and MS degrees from California State University at San Francisco.

Lavaroni was the owner-operator of the Kittredge School, a very successful, small independent elementary school in San Francisco. While at Kittredge he founded and was the first president of the National Independent Private Schools Association

(NIPSA), recognized by the US Office of Education as the accrediting agency of for-profit elementary and secondary schools.

Lavaroni has authored and coauthored several textbooks as well as many articles and papers. He has served as a consultant for programs in critical thinking, inquiry training, assessment and evaluation, and individualized instruction throughout the US and eight foreign countries. He has also been involved in developing five corporations focusing on education. Currently, he is codirector, with Leisey, of the International Academy for Educational Entrepreneurship.

# We Want Your Thoughts

After you have read and reflected on the profiles of the educational entrepreneurs featured in this book, we hope you will share your reactions with us. Please let us know of other educational entrepreneurs you think are worthy of including in future publications.

Further, if you are considering taking the plunge into becoming an educational entrepreneur, we would enjoy hearing from you. The mission of the International Academy for Educational Entrepreneurship (IAEE) is to encourage and support educators who have already invested or are interested in investing time, energy, and capital to create, develop, and market programs, products, services and/or technologies designed to enhance and improve education. We envision the establishment of a network of people who will be available to encourage and assist educational entrepreneurs in the process of creating and maintaining new and exciting educational programs, products, services, and technologies.

It is our fervent hope that the Academy can assist *you* in making a difference in education.

*Donald E. Leisey, EdD*
*Charles W. Lavaroni, MS*


**International Academy for Educational Entrepreneurship**

Del Tower
21 Silk Oak Circle
San Rafael, CA 94901

Phone: 415-454-0217
Fax: 415-459-4057
E-mail: edentrepreneurs@aol.com


Visit our Web site at www.edentrepreneurs.org

If you liked this book and want to purchase one for someone else, please check with your local bookstore or online bookseller, or use this form:

Name ______________________________________________

Organization ________________________________________

Address ____________________________________________

City ______________________ State _____ Zip ____________

*The Educational Entrepreneur* ____ copies @ $14.95 each $ _______

California residents, please add applicable sales tax $ _______

Shipping: $3.20/first copy; $1.60 each additional copy* $ _______

Total enclosed, or charge my credit card $ _______

Payment by: ☐ Check ☐ Credit Card ☐ Purchase Order**

Credit Card Number: ______________________________

Expiration Date: _________________________________

☐ MasterCard ☐ Visa ☐ American Express

For more than 5 copies, please contact the publisher for quantity rates. Send completed order form and your payment or purchase order to:

Edupreneur Press
DEL Tower
21 Silk Oak Circle
San Rafael, CA 94901
Phone: 415-454-0217
Fax: 415-459-4057
E-mail: edentrepreneurs@aol.com

or order via our Web site at **www.edentrepreneurs.org**

*For international shipping rates, please contact the publisher.

**Only purchase orders from recognized educational institutions or government agencies will be honored.